CONTENTS

1.ARRAY OPERATIONS

1.1. Create, Initialize elements, Insert element, Delete element & Search element in an array

Below is a simple example of a Java class that demonstrates creating an array, initializing its elements, inserting an element, deleting an element, and searching for an element.

```
public class ArrayOperations {
   private int[] array;
   private int size;
   private static final int DEFAULT_CAPACITY = 10;
   // Constructor to initialize the array with a default capacity
   public ArrayOperations() {
      array = new int[DEFAULT_CAPACITY];
      size = 0;
   }
   // Method to display the elements of the array
   public void display() {
      System.out.print("Array Elements: ");
      for (int i = 0; i < size; i++) {
         System.out.print(array[i] + " ");
      }
      System.out.println();
   }
   // Method to insert an element at the end of the array
   public void insertElement(int element) {
      if (size == array.length) {
         // If the array is full, double its capacity
         int[] newArray = new int[array.length * 2];
         System.arraycopy(array, 0, newArray, 0, size);
         array = newArray;
      }
      array[size] = element;
      size++;
```

```
}
// Method to delete an element from the array
public void deleteElement(int element) {
    int index = searchElement(element);
    if (index != -1) {
        // Shift elements to the left to fill the gap
        for (int i = index; i < size - 1; i++) {
            array[i] = array[i + 1];
        }
        size--;
    } else {
        System.out.println("Element not found in the array.");
    }
}
// Method to search for an element in the array
public int searchElement(int element) {
    for (int i = 0; i < size; i++) {
        if (array[i] == element) {
            return i; // Return the index if the element is found
        }
    }
    return -1; // Return -1 if the element is not found
}
public static void main(String[] args) {
    ArrayOperations arrayOps = new ArrayOperations();
    // Insert elements into the array
    arrayOps.insertElement(10);
    arrayOps.insertElement(20);
    arrayOps.insertElement(30);
    arrayOps.display();

    // Search for an element in the array
    int searchResult = arrayOps.searchElement(20);
```

```
        System.out.println("Search Result: Element 20 found at index " + searchResult);
        // Delete an element from the array
        arrayOps.deleteElement(20);
        arrayOps.display();
    }
}
```

1.2. Sum elements in an array

Below is an example of a Java class that calculates the sum of elements in an array:

```
public class ArraySumCalculator {
    private int[] array;
    private int size;
    // Constructor to initialize the array
    public ArraySumCalculator(int[] array) {
        this.array = array;
        this.size = array.length;
    }
    // Method to calculate the sum of elements in the array
    public int calculateSum() {
        int sum = 0;
        for (int i = 0; i < size; i++) {
            sum += array[i];
        }
        return sum;
    }
    public static void main(String[] args) {
        // Example usage
        int[] exampleArray = {5, 10, 15, 20, 25};
        ArraySumCalculator sumCalculator = new ArraySumCalculator(exampleArray);
        // Calculate and display the sum of elements
        int result = sumCalculator.calculateSum();
        System.out.println("Sum of elements in the array: " + result);
    }
}
```

In this example, the ArraySumCalculator class takes an array as a parameter in its constructor. The calculateSum method iterates through the elements of the array, adding them up to calculate the sum. The main method demonstrates how to create an instance of the class and use it to calculate the sum of elements in an example array.

1.3.Average elements in an array

Here's an example of a Java class that calculates the average of elements in an array:

```
public class ArrayAverageCalculator {
    private int[] array;
    private int size;
    // Constructor to initialize the array
    public ArrayAverageCalculator(int[] array) {
        this.array = array;
        this.size = array.length;
    }
    // Method to calculate the average of elements in the array
    public double calculateAverage() {
        if (size == 0) {
            return 0; // Avoid division by zero
        }
        int sum = 0;
        for (int i = 0; i < size; i++) {
            sum += array[i];
        }
        return (double) sum / size;
    }
    public static void main(String[] args) {
        // Example usage
        int[] exampleArray = {5, 10, 15, 20, 25};
        ArrayAverageCalculator averageCalculator = new
ArrayAverageCalculator(exampleArray);
        // Calculate and display the average of elements
        double result = averageCalculator.calculateAverage();
        System.out.println("Average of elements in the array: " + result);
    }
}
```

In this example, the ArrayAverageCalculator class takes an array as a parameter in its constructor. The calculateAverage method first checks if the array is empty to avoid division by zero. Then, it calculates the sum of elements and divides it by the size of the array to find the average. The main method demonstrates how to create an instance of the class and use it to calculate the average of elements in an example array.

You can replace the exampleArray with your own array or integrate the calculateAverage method into an existing class structure as needed.

1.4. Find the maximum element in an array

Here's an example of a Java class that finds the maximum element in an array:

```
public class ArrayMaxFinder {
    private int[] array;
    private int size;
    // Constructor to initialize the array
    public ArrayMaxFinder(int[] array) {
        this.array = array;
        this.size = array.length;
    }
    // Method to find the maximum element in the array
    public int findMax() {
        if (size == 0) {
            throw new IllegalArgumentException("Array is empty");
        }
        int max = array[0];
        for (int i = 1; i < size; i++) {
            if (array[i] > max) {
                max = array[i];
            }
        }
        return max;
    }
    public static void main(String[] args) {
        // Example usage
        int[] exampleArray = {5, 10, 15, 20, 25};
        ArrayMaxFinder maxFinder = new ArrayMaxFinder(exampleArray);
        // Find and display the maximum element in the array
        int result = maxFinder.findMax();
        System.out.println("Maximum element in the array: " + result);
    }
}
```

In this example, the ArrayMaxFinder class takes an array as a parameter in its constructor. The findMax method iterates through the elements of the array, keeping track of the maximum element. The main method demonstrates how to create an instance of the class and use it to find the maximum element in an example array.

You can replace the exampleArray with your own array or integrate the findMax method into an existing class structure as needed.

1.5. Find the minimum element in an array

Below is an example of a Java class that finds the minimum element in an array:

```
public class ArrayMinFinder {
    private int[] array;
    private int size;
    // Constructor to initialize the array
    public ArrayMinFinder(int[] array) {
        this.array = array;
        this.size = array.length;
    }
    // Method to find the minimum element in the array
    public int findMin() {
        if (size == 0) {
            throw new IllegalArgumentException("Array is empty");
        }
        int min = array[0];
        for (int i = 1; i < size; i++) {
            if (array[i] < min) {
                min = array[i];
            }
        }
        return min;
    }
    public static void main(String[] args) {
        // Example usage
        int[] exampleArray = {5, 10, 15, 20, 25};
        ArrayMinFinder minFinder = new ArrayMinFinder(exampleArray);
        // Find and display the minimum element in the array
        int result = minFinder.findMin();
        System.out.println("Minimum element in the array: " + result);
    }}
```

In this example, the ArrayMinFinder class takes an array as a parameter in its constructor. The findMin method iterates through the elements of the array, keeping track of the minimum element. The main method demonstrates how to create an instance of the class and use it to find the minimum element in an example array.

You can replace the exampleArray with your own array or integrate the findMin method into an existing class structure as needed.

1.6. Merge two sorted Arrays

Below is an example of a Java class that merges two sorted arrays into a single sorted array:

```
public class ArrayMerger {
   private int[] array1;
   private int[] array2;
   private int size1;
   private int size2;
   // Constructor to initialize the arrays
   public ArrayMerger(int[] array1, int[] array2) {
      this.array1 = array1;
      this.array2 = array2;
      this.size1 = array1.length;
      this.size2 = array2.length;
   }
   // Method to merge two sorted arrays into a single sorted array
   public int[] mergeArrays() {
      int[] mergedArray = new int[size1 + size2];
      int i = 0, j = 0, k = 0;
      while (i < size1 && j < size2) {
         if (array1[i] < array2[j]) {
            mergedArray[k++] = array1[i++];
         } else {
            mergedArray[k++] = array2[j++];
         }
      }
      // Copy the remaining elements from array1, if any
      while (i < size1) {
         mergedArray[k++] = array1[i++];
      }
      // Copy the remaining elements from array2, if any
      while (j < size2) {
         mergedArray[k++] = array2[j++];
```

```
        }
        return mergedArray;
    }
    public static void main(String[] args) {
        // Example usage
        int[] sortedArray1 = {1, 3, 5, 7, 9};
        int[] sortedArray2 = {2, 4, 6, 8, 10};
        ArrayMerger merger = new ArrayMerger(sortedArray1, sortedArray2);
        // Merge and display the sorted array
        int[] result = merger.mergeArrays();
        System.out.print("Merged Sorted Array: ");
        for (int value : result) {
            System.out.print(value + " ");
        }
    }
}
```

In this example, the ArrayMerger class takes two sorted arrays as parameters in its constructor. The mergeArrays method then merges the arrays into a new sorted array. The main method demonstrates how to create an instance of the class and use it to merge two sorted arrays.

You can replace the sortedArray1 and sortedArray2 with your own sorted arrays or integrate the mergeArrays method into an existing class structure as needed.

2.SEARCHING TECHNIQUES

2.1.Binary search

Below is an example of a Java class that performs a binary search on a sorted array:

```
public class BinarySearch {
    private int[] array;
    private int size;
    // Constructor to initialize the array
    public BinarySearch(int[] array) {
        // Assuming the input array is already sorted
        this.array = array;
        this.size = array.length;
    }
    // Method to perform binary search and return the index of the target element
    // Returns -1 if the element is not found
    public int binarySearch(int target) {
        int low = 0;
        int high = size - 1;
        while (low <= high) {
            int mid = low + (high - low) / 2;
            if (array[mid] == target) {
                return mid; // Element found, return its index
            } else if (array[mid] < target) {
                low = mid + 1; // Discard the left half
            } else {
                high = mid - 1; // Discard the right half
            }
        }
        return -1; // Element not found
    }
    public static void main(String[] args) {
        // Example usage
        int[] sortedArray = {1, 3, 5, 7, 9, 11, 13, 15, 17, 19};
        BinarySearch binarySearch = new BinarySearch(sortedArray);
```

```
        // Perform binary search and display the result
        int targetElement = 15;
        int result = binarySearch.binarySearch(targetElement);
        if (result != -1) {
            System.out.println("Element " + targetElement + " found at index " + result);
        } else {
            System.out.println("Element " + targetElement + " not found in the array.");
        }
    }
}
```

In this example, the BinarySearch class takes a sorted array as a parameter in its constructor. The binarySearch method performs the binary search algorithm to find the index of a target element. The main method demonstrates how to create an instance of the class and use it to perform a binary search on a sorted array.

You can replace the sortedArray with your own sorted array or integrate the binarySearch method into an existing class structure as needed.

2.2.Linear search

Here's an example of a Java class that performs linear search on an array:

```
public class LinearSearch {
    private int[] array;
    private int size;
    // Constructor to initialize the array
    public LinearSearch(int[] array) {
        this.array = array;
        this.size = array.length;
    }
    // Method to perform linear search and return the index of the target element
    // Returns -1 if the element is not found
    public int linearSearch(int target) {
        for (int i = 0; i < size; i++) {
            if (array[i] == target) {
                return i; // Element found, return its index
            }
        }
        return -1; // Element not found
    }
    public static void main(String[] args) {
        // Example usage
        int[] array = {5, 8, 2, 10, 15, 7, 3};
        LinearSearch linearSearch = new LinearSearch(array);
        // Perform linear search and display the result
        int targetElement = 15;
        int result = linearSearch.linearSearch(targetElement);
        if (result != -1) {
            System.out.println("Element " + targetElement + " found at index " + result);
        } else {
            System.out.println("Element " + targetElement + " not found in the array.");
        }
    }
```

```
}
```

In this example, the LinearSearch class takes an array as a parameter in its constructor. The linearSearch method performs the linear search algorithm to find the index of a target element. The main method demonstrates how to create an instance of the class and use it to perform a linear search on an array.

You can replace the array with your own array or integrate the linearSearch method into an existing class structure as needed.

2.3.Quadratic probing

Quadratic probing is a technique used in open-addressing hash tables to resolve collisions. Here's an example of a Java class that implements quadratic probing for a simple hash table:

```
public class QuadraticProbingHashTable {
    private int capacity;
    private int[] table;
    public QuadraticProbingHashTable(int capacity) {
        this.capacity = capacity;
        this.table = new int[capacity];
    }
    // Method to insert a key into the hash table using quadratic probing
    public void insert(int key) {
        int hash = hashFunction(key);
        int index = hash;
        int i = 1;
        while (table[index] != 0) {
            // Quadratic probing: increment index by i^2
            index = (hash + i * i) % capacity;
            i++;
            if (i > capacity) {
                System.out.println("Hash table is full. Unable to insert key: " + key);
                return;
            }
        }
        table[index] = key;
    }
    // Method to perform a basic hash function
    private int hashFunction(int key) {
        return key % capacity;
    }
    // Method to display the contents of the hash table
    public void display() {
```

```
        System.out.print("Hash Table: ");
        for (int value : table) {
            System.out.print(value + " ");
        }
        System.out.println();
    }
    public static void main(String[] args) {
        // Example usage
        QuadraticProbingHashTable hashTable = new QuadraticProbingHashTable(10);
        // Insert keys into the hash table
        hashTable.insert(5);
        hashTable.insert(15);
        hashTable.insert(25);
        hashTable.insert(35);
        hashTable.insert(45);
        // Display the contents of the hash table
        hashTable.display();
    }
}
```

In this example, the QuadraticProbingHashTable class uses quadratic probing to resolve collisions during the insertion of keys into the hash table. The insert method calculates the next index using the quadratic probing formula (index = (hash + i^2) % capacity) until an empty slot is found. The hashFunction method provides a simple hash function for demonstration purposes. The display method is used to print the contents of the hash table.

You can modify the main method and add more keys to test the quadratic probing implementation.

2.4. Linear Probing

Below is an example of a Java class that implements linear probing for a simple hash table:

```
public class LinearProbingHashTable {
    private int capacity;
    private int[] table;
    public LinearProbingHashTable(int capacity) {
        this.capacity = capacity;
        this.table = new int[capacity];
    }
    // Method to insert a key into the hash table using linear probing
    public void insert(int key) {
        int hash = hashFunction(key);
        int index = hash;
        while (table[index] != 0) {
            // Linear probing: increment index by 1
            index = (index + 1) % capacity;
        }
        table[index] = key;
    }
    // Method to perform a basic hash function
    private int hashFunction(int key) {
        return key % capacity;
    }
    // Method to display the contents of the hash table
    public void display() {
        System.out.print("Hash Table: ");
        for (int value : table) {
            System.out.print(value + " ");
        }
        System.out.println();
    }
    public static void main(String[] args) {
```

```
        // Example usage
        LinearProbingHashTable hashTable = new LinearProbingHashTable(10);
        // Insert keys into the hash table
        hashTable.insert(5);
        hashTable.insert(15);
        hashTable.insert(25);
        hashTable.insert(35);
        hashTable.insert(45);
        // Display the contents of the hash table
        hashTable.display();
    }
}
```

In this example, the LinearProbingHashTable class uses linear probing to resolve collisions during the insertion of keys into the hash table. The insert method calculates the next index using linear probing by incrementing the index by 1 until an empty slot is found. The hashFunction method provides a simple hash function for demonstration purposes. The display method is used to print the contents of the hash table.

You can modify the main method and add more keys to test the linear probing implementation.

3.LINKED LIST

3.1. Create, insert, delete and display operations

Below is an example of a Java class that defines a basic linked list with operations to create, insert, delete, and display elements:

```
class Node {
    int data;
    Node next;
    public Node(int data) {
        this.data = data;
        this.next = null;
    }
}
public class LinkedList {
    private Node head;
    // Constructor to initialize an empty linked list
    public LinkedList() {
        this.head = null;
    }
    // Method to insert a new element at the end of the linked list
    public void insert(int data) {
        Node newNode = new Node(data);
        if (head == null) {
            head = newNode;
        } else {
            Node current = head;
            while (current.next != null) {
                current = current.next;
            }
            current.next = newNode;
        }
    }
    // Method to delete an element from the linked list
    public void delete(int data) {
```

```
        if (head == null) {
            System.out.println("Cannot delete from an empty list.");
            return;
        }
        if (head.data == data) {
            head = head.next;
            return;
        }
        Node current = head;
        Node prev = null;
        while (current != null && current.data != data) {
            prev = current;
            current = current.next;
        }
        if (current == null) {
            System.out.println("Element not found in the list.");
            return;
        }
        prev.next = current.next;
    }
    // Method to display the elements of the linked list
    public void display() {
        Node current = head;
        System.out.print("Linked List: ");
        while (current != null) {
            System.out.print(current.data + " ");
            current = current.next;
        }
        System.out.println();
    }
    public static void main(String[] args) {
        // Example usage
        LinkedList linkedList = new LinkedList();
```

```
        // Insert elements into the linked list
        linkedList.insert(5);
        linkedList.insert(10);
        linkedList.insert(15);
        linkedList.insert(20);
        // Display the initial linked list
        linkedList.display();
        // Delete an element from the linked list
        linkedList.delete(10);
        // Display the modified linked list
        linkedList.display();
    }
}
```

In this example, the Node class represents a node in the linked list, and the LinkedList class contains methods for creating, inserting, deleting, and displaying elements in the linked list. The main method demonstrates the basic usage of these operations. You can modify the main method and add more elements to test the linked list implementation.

3.2. Perform traversal

Below is an example of a Java class that performs traversal (both forward and backward) on a linked list:

```
class Node {
    int data;
    Node next;
    Node prev; // For doubly linked list
    public Node(int data) {
        this.data = data;
        this.next = null;
        this.prev = null;
    }
}
public class LinkedList {
    private Node head;
    // Constructor to initialize an empty linked list
    public LinkedList() {
        this.head = null;
    }
    // Method to insert a new element at the end of the linked list
    public void insert(int data) {
        Node newNode = new Node(data);
        if (head == null) {
            head = newNode;
        } else {
            Node current = head;
            while (current.next != null) {
                current = current.next;
            }
            current.next = newNode;
            newNode.prev = current; // For doubly linked list
        }
    }
```

```
// Method to perform forward traversal and display the elements of the linked list
public void forwardTraversal() {
    Node current = head;
    System.out.print("Forward Traversal: ");
    while (current != null) {
        System.out.print(current.data + " ");
        current = current.next;
    }
    System.out.println();
}
// Method to perform backward traversal and display the elements of the linked list
public void backwardTraversal() {
    Node current = head;
    if (current == null) {
        System.out.println("Cannot perform backward traversal on an empty list.");
        return;
    }
    // Move to the end of the list
    while (current.next != null) {
        current = current.next;
    }
    System.out.print("Backward Traversal: ");
    while (current != null) {
        System.out.print(current.data + " ");
        current = current.prev; // For doubly linked list
    }
    System.out.println();
}
```

```
    public static void main(String[] args) {
        // Example usage
        LinkedList linkedList = new LinkedList();
        // Insert elements into the linked list
        linkedList.insert(5);
        linkedList.insert(10);
        linkedList.insert(15);
        linkedList.insert(20);
        // Perform forward traversal and display the elements
        linkedList.forwardTraversal();
        // Perform backward traversal and display the elements (for doubly linked list)
        linkedList.backwardTraversal();
    }
}
```

In this example, the Node class represents a node in the linked list, and the LinkedList class contains methods for inserting elements and performing both forward and backward traversal. The main method demonstrates the basic usage of these operations. You can modify the main method and add more elements to test the linked list implementation. Note that the backward traversal is implemented assuming a doubly linked list, which includes a prev pointer in each node. If you're working with a singly linked list, the backward traversal would not be possible in the same way.

3.3. Implement a singly linked list

Below is an example of a Java class that implements a singly linked list with operations for inserting, deleting, displaying, and searching elements:

```
class Node {
    int data;
    Node next;
    public Node(int data) {
        this.data = data;
        this.next = null;
    }
}
public class SinglyLinkedList {
    private Node head;
    // Constructor to initialize an empty linked list
    public SinglyLinkedList() {
        this.head = null;
    }
    // Method to insert a new element at the end of the linked list
    public void insert(int data) {
        Node newNode = new Node(data);
        if (head == null) {
            head = newNode;
        } else {
            Node current = head;
            while (current.next != null) {
                current = current.next;
            }
            current.next = newNode;
        }
    }
    // Method to delete an element from the linked list
    public void delete(int data) {
        if (head == null) {
```

```
            System.out.println("Cannot delete from an empty list.");
            return;
        }
        if (head.data == data) {
            head = head.next;
            return;
        }
        Node current = head;
        Node prev = null;
        while (current != null && current.data != data) {
            prev = current;
            current = current.next;
        }
        if (current == null) {
            System.out.println("Element not found in the list.");
            return;
        }
        prev.next = current.next;
    }
    // Method to display the elements of the linked list
    public void display() {
        Node current = head;
        System.out.print("Linked List: ");
        while (current != null) {
            System.out.print(current.data + " ");
            current = current.next;
        }
        System.out.println();
    }

    // Method to search for an element in the linked list
    public boolean search(int data) {
        Node current = head;
```

```
        while (current != null) {
            if (current.data == data) {
                return true; // Element found
            }
            current = current.next;
        }
        return false; // Element not found
    }
    public static void main(String[] args) {
        // Example usage
        SinglyLinkedList linkedList = new SinglyLinkedList();
        // Insert elements into the linked list
        linkedList.insert(5);
        linkedList.insert(10);
        linkedList.insert(15);
        linkedList.insert(20);
        // Display the initial linked list
        linkedList.display();
        // Search for an element in the linked list
        int searchElement = 10;
        if (linkedList.search(searchElement)) {
            System.out.println("Element " + searchElement + " found in the list.");
        } else {
            System.out.println("Element " + searchElement + " not found in the list.");
        }
        // Delete an element from the linked list
        linkedList.delete(10);

        // Display the modified linked list
        linkedList.display();
    }
}
```

In this example, the Node class represents a node in the singly linked list, and the SinglyLinkedList class contains methods for inserting, deleting, displaying, and searching elements in the linked list. The main method demonstrates the basic usage of these operations. You can modify the main method and add more elements to test the linked list implementation.

3.4. Implement a doubly linked list

Below is an example of a Java class that implements a doubly linked list with operations for inserting, deleting, displaying, and searching elements:

```
class Node {
   int data;
   Node next;
   Node prev;
   public Node(int data) {
      this.data = data;
      this.next = null;
      this.prev = null;
   }
}
public class DoublyLinkedList {
   private Node head;
   // Constructor to initialize an empty doubly linked list
   public DoublyLinkedList() {
      this.head = null;
   }
   // Method to insert a new element at the end of the doubly linked list
   public void insert(int data) {
      Node newNode = new Node(data);
      if (head == null) {
         head = newNode;
      } else {
         Node current = head;
         while (current.next != null) {
            current = current.next;
         }
         current.next = newNode;
         newNode.prev = current;
      }
   }
```

```
// Method to delete an element from the doubly linked list
public void delete(int data) {
    if (head == null) {
        System.out.println("Cannot delete from an empty list.");
        return;
    }
    if (head.data == data) {
        head = head.next;
        if (head != null) {
            head.prev = null;
        }
        return;
    }
    Node current = head;
    while (current != null && current.data != data) {
        current = current.next;
    }
    if (current == null) {
        System.out.println("Element not found in the list.");
        return;
    }
    if (current.next != null) {
        current.next.prev = current.prev;
    }
    current.prev.next = current.next;
}
// Method to display the elements of the doubly linked list
public void display() {
    Node current = head;

    System.out.print("Doubly Linked List (Forward): ");
    while (current != null) {
        System.out.print(current.data + " ");
```

```
            current = current.next;
        }
        System.out.println();
        // Display in reverse order
        System.out.print("Doubly Linked List (Backward): ");
        while (current != null) {
            System.out.print(current.data + " ");
            current = current.prev;
        }
        System.out.println();
    }
    // Method to search for an element in the doubly linked list
    public boolean search(int data) {
        Node current = head;
        while (current != null) {
            if (current.data == data) {
                return true; // Element found
            }
            current = current.next;
        }
        return false; // Element not found
    }
    public static void main(String[] args) {
        // Example usage
        DoublyLinkedList doublyLinkedList = new DoublyLinkedList();
        // Insert elements into the doubly linked list
        doublyLinkedList.insert(5);
        doublyLinkedList.insert(10);
        doublyLinkedList.insert(15);
        doublyLinkedList.insert(20);
        // Display the initial doubly linked list
        doublyLinkedList.display();
        // Search for an element in the doubly linked list
```

```
        int searchElement = 10;
        if (doublyLinkedList.search(searchElement)) {
            System.out.println("Element " + searchElement + " found in the list.");
        } else {
            System.out.println("Element " + searchElement + " not found in the list.");
        }
        // Delete an element from the doubly linked list
        doublyLinkedList.delete(10);
        // Display the modified doubly linked list
        doublyLinkedList.display();
    }
}
```

In this example, the Node class represents a node in the doubly linked list, and the DoublyLinkedList class contains methods for inserting, deleting, displaying, and searching elements in the doubly linked list. The main method demonstrates the basic usage of these operations. You can modify the main method and add more elements to test the doubly linked list implementation.

3.5.Reverse a linked list

Below is an example of a Java class that reverses a singly linked list:

```
class Node {
    int data;
    Node next;
    public Node(int data) {
        this.data = data;
        this.next = null;
    }
}
public class ReverseLinkedList {
    private Node head;
    // Constructor to initialize an empty linked list
    public ReverseLinkedList() {
        this.head = null;
    }
    // Method to insert a new element at the end of the linked list
    public void insert(int data) {
        Node newNode = new Node(data);
        if (head == null) {
            head = newNode;
        } else {
            Node current = head;
            while (current.next != null) {
                current = current.next;
            }
            current.next = newNode;
        }
    }
    // Method to reverse the linked list
    public void reverse() {
        Node prev = null;
        Node current = head;
```

```
        Node next = null;
        while (current != null) {
            next = current.next; // Save the next node
            current.next = prev; // Reverse the link
            prev = current; // Move prev to the current node
            current = next; // Move current to the next node
        }
        head = prev; // Update the head to the last node
    }
    // Method to display the elements of the linked list
    public void display() {
        Node current = head;
        System.out.print("Linked List: ");
        while (current != null) {
            System.out.print(current.data + " ");
            current = current.next;
        }
        System.out.println();
    }
    public static void main(String[] args) {
        // Example usage
        ReverseLinkedList linkedList = new ReverseLinkedList();
        // Insert elements into the linked list
        linkedList.insert(5);
        linkedList.insert(10);
        linkedList.insert(15);
        linkedList.insert(20);
        // Display the initial linked list
        System.out.println("Original Linked List:");
        linkedList.display();
        // Reverse the linked list
        linkedList.reverse();
        // Display the reversed linked list
```

```
        System.out.println("\nReversed Linked List:");
        linkedList.display();
    }
}
```

In this example, the ReverseLinkedList class contains a reverse method that reverses the order of nodes in the linked list. The main method demonstrates how to create a linked list, insert elements, display the original list, reverse it, and then display the reversed list. You can modify the main method and add more elements to test the reverse operation on the linked list.

3.6.Detecting loop in a linked list

Below is an example of a Java class that detects a loop in a linked list using Floyd's Cycle Detection Algorithm:

```
class Node {
    int data;
    Node next;
    public Node(int data) {
        this.data = data;
        this.next = null;
    }
}
public class DetectLoop {
    private Node head;
    // Constructor to initialize an empty linked list
    public DetectLoop() {
        this.head = null;
    }
    // Method to insert a new element at the end of the linked list
    public void insert(int data) {
        Node newNode = new Node(data);
        if (head == null) {
            head = newNode;
        } else {
            Node current = head;
            while (current.next != null) {
                current = current.next;
            }
            current.next = newNode;
        }
    }
    // Method to detect a loop in the linked list using Floyd's Cycle Detection Algorithm
    public boolean detectLoop() {
        Node slow = head;
```

```
        Node fast = head;
        while (fast != null && fast.next != null) {
            slow = slow.next;
            fast = fast.next.next;
            if (slow == fast) {
                return true; // Loop detected
            }
        }
        return false; // No loop
    }
    // Method to display the elements of the linked list
    public void display() {
        Node current = head;
        System.out.print("Linked List: ");
        while (current != null) {
            System.out.print(current.data + " ");
            current = current.next;
        }
        System.out.println();
    }
    public static void main(String[] args) {
        // Example usage
        DetectLoop linkedList = new DetectLoop();
        // Insert elements into the linked list
        linkedList.insert(5);
        linkedList.insert(10);
        linkedList.insert(15);
        linkedList.insert(20);

        // Display the initial linked list
        linkedList.display();
        // Detect loop (none in this case)
        boolean loopDetected = linkedList.detectLoop();
```

```
        System.out.println("Loop Detected: " + loopDetected);
        // Create a loop for testing
        linkedList.head.next.next.next.next = linkedList.head.next; // Creating a loop
        // Detect loop (now there is a loop)
        loopDetected = linkedList.detectLoop();
        System.out.println("Loop Detected: " + loopDetected);
    }
}
```

In this example, the DetectLoop class contains a detectLoop method that uses Floyd's Cycle Detection Algorithm to check for a loop in the linked list. The main method demonstrates how to create a linked list, insert elements, display the list, and detect the presence of a loop. You can modify the main method and add more elements to test the loop detection on the linked list.

3.7. Removing loops in a linked list

To remove loops in a linked list, you can modify the previous example and add a method to detect and remove the loop. Here's an example of a Java class that removes loops in a linked list:

```
class Node {
    int data;
    Node next;
    public Node(int data) {
        this.data = data;
        this.next = null;
    }
}
public class RemoveLoop {
    private Node head;
    // Constructor to initialize an empty linked list
    public RemoveLoop() {
        this.head = null;
    }
    // Method to insert a new element at the end of the linked list
    public void insert(int data) {
        Node newNode = new Node(data);
        if (head == null) {
            head = newNode;
        } else {
            Node current = head;
            while (current.next != null) {
                current = current.next;
            }
            current.next = newNode;
        }
    }
    // Method to detect and remove a loop in the linked list using Floyd's Cycle Detection
Algorithm
```

```
public void detectAndRemoveLoop() {
    Node slow = head;
    Node fast = head;
    Node prev = null;
    while (fast != null && fast.next != null) {
        slow = slow.next;
        fast = fast.next.next;
        if (slow == fast) {
            removeLoop(slow, head);
            return;
        }
    }
}
// Helper method to remove the loop in the linked list
private void removeLoop(Node loopNode, Node head) {
    Node ptr1 = head;
    Node ptr2 = loopNode;
    // Move one pointer to the head
    while (ptr1.next != ptr2.next) {
        ptr1 = ptr1.next;
        ptr2 = ptr2.next;
    }
    // Set the next of the loop node to null to remove the loop
    ptr2.next = null;
}
// Method to display the elements of the linked list
public void display() {
    Node current = head;
    System.out.print("Linked List: ");
    while (current != null) {
        System.out.print(current.data + " ");
        current = current.next;
    }
```

```
        System.out.println();
    }
    public static void main(String[] args) {
        // Example usage
        RemoveLoop linkedList = new RemoveLoop();
        // Insert elements into the linked list
        linkedList.insert(5);
        linkedList.insert(10);
        linkedList.insert(15);
        linkedList.insert(20);
        // Create a loop for testing
        linkedList.head.next.next.next.next = linkedList.head.next; // Creating a loop
        // Detect and remove loop
        linkedList.detectAndRemoveLoop();
        // Display the modified linked list
        linkedList.display();
    }
}
```

In this example, the detectAndRemoveLoop method uses Floyd's Cycle Detection Algorithm to detect the loop, and the removeLoop helper method is used to remove the loop. The main method demonstrates how to create a linked list, insert elements, display the list, create a loop, detect and remove the loop, and then display the modified list. You can modify the main method and add more elements to test the loop detection and removal on the linked list.

4. SORTING

4.1. Bubble sort

Below is an example of a Java class that implements the bubble sort algorithm:

```
public class BubbleSort {
   private int[] array;
   public BubbleSort(int[] array) {
      this.array = array;
   }
   // Method to perform bubble sort on the array
   public void sort() {
      int n = array.length;
      for (int i = 0; i < n - 1; i++) {
         for (int j = 0; j < n - i - 1; j++) {
            // Compare adjacent elements and swap if necessary
            if (array[j] > array[j + 1]) {
               int temp = array[j];
               array[j] = array[j + 1];
               array[j + 1] = temp;
            }
         }
      }
   }
   // Method to display the sorted array
   public void display() {
      System.out.print("Sorted Array: ");
      for (int value : array) {
         System.out.print(value + " ");
      }
      System.out.println();
   }
   public static void main(String[] args) {
      // Example usage
      int[] array = {64, 34, 25, 12, 22, 11, 90};
```

```
        BubbleSort bubbleSort = new BubbleSort(array);
        // Display the original array
        System.out.print("Original Array: ");
        for (int value : array) {
            System.out.print(value + " ");
        }
        System.out.println();
        // Perform bubble sort
        bubbleSort.sort();
        // Display the sorted array
        bubbleSort.display();
    }
}
```

In this example, the BubbleSort class takes an array as a parameter in its constructor and contains a sort method to perform the bubble sort algorithm. The display method is used to print the sorted array. The main method demonstrates how to create an instance of the class, display the original array, perform the bubble sort, and then display the sorted array.

You can replace the array in the main method with your own array or integrate the sort method into an existing class structure as needed.

4.2.Selection sort

Below is an example of a Java class that implements the selection sort algorithm:

```
public class SelectionSort {
  private int[] array;
  public SelectionSort(int[] array) {
    this.array = array;
  }
  // Method to perform selection sort on the array
  public void sort() {
    int n = array.length;
    for (int i = 0; i < n - 1; i++) {
      // Find the minimum element in the unsorted part of the array
      int minIndex = i;
      for (int j = i + 1; j < n; j++) {
        if (array[j] < array[minIndex]) {
          minIndex = j;
        }
      }
      // Swap the found minimum element with the first element
      int temp = array[minIndex];
      array[minIndex] = array[i];
      array[i] = temp;
    }
  }
  // Method to display the sorted array
  public void display() {
    System.out.print("Sorted Array: ");
    for (int value : array) {
      System.out.print(value + " ");
    }
    System.out.println();
  }
```

```
    public static void main(String[] args) {
        // Example usage
        int[] array = {64, 34, 25, 12, 22, 11, 90};
        SelectionSort selectionSort = new SelectionSort(array);
        // Display the original array
        System.out.print("Original Array: ");
        for (int value : array) {
            System.out.print(value + " ");
        }
        System.out.println();
        // Perform selection sort
        selectionSort.sort();
        // Display the sorted array
        selectionSort.display();
    }
}
```

In this example, the SelectionSort class takes an array as a parameter in its constructor and contains a sort method to perform the selection sort algorithm. The display method is used to print the sorted array. The main method demonstrates how to create an instance of the class, display the original array, perform the selection sort, and then display the sorted array.

You can replace the array in the main method with your own array or integrate the sort method into an existing class structure as needed.

4.3.Insertion sort

Below is an example of a Java class that implements the insertion sort algorithm:

```
public class InsertionSort {
    private int[] array;
    public InsertionSort(int[] array) {
        this.array = array;
    }
    // Method to perform insertion sort on the array
    public void sort() {
        int n = array.length;
        for (int i = 1; i < n; i++) {
            int key = array[i];
            int j = i - 1;
            // Move elements of array[0..i-1] that are greater than key to one position ahead of
their current position
            while (j >= 0 && array[j] > key) {
                array[j + 1] = array[j];
                j = j - 1;
            }
            array[j + 1] = key;
        }
    }
    // Method to display the sorted array
    public void display() {
        System.out.print("Sorted Array: ");
        for (int value : array) {
            System.out.print(value + " ");
        }
        System.out.println();
    }
    public static void main(String[] args) {
        // Example usage
        int[] array = {64, 34, 25, 12, 22, 11, 90};
```

```
        InsertionSort insertionSort = new InsertionSort(array);
        // Display the original array
        System.out.print("Original Array: ");
        for (int value : array) {
            System.out.print(value + " ");
        }
        System.out.println();
        // Perform insertion sort
        insertionSort.sort();
        // Display the sorted array
        insertionSort.display();
    }
}
```

In this example, the InsertionSort class takes an array as a parameter in its constructor and contains a sort method to perform the insertion sort algorithm. The display method is used to print the sorted array. The main method demonstrates how to create an instance of the class, display the original array, perform the insertion sort, and then display the sorted array.

You can replace the array in the main method with your own array or integrate the sort method into an existing class structure as needed.

4.4. Merge sort

Below is an example of a Java class that implements the merge sort algorithm:

```
public class MergeSort {
    private int[] array;
    public MergeSort(int[] array) {
        this.array = array;
    }
    // Method to perform merge sort on the array
    public void sort() {
        mergeSort(0, array.length - 1);
    }
    // Recursive method to perform merge sort
    private void mergeSort(int low, int high) {
        if (low < high) {
            // Find the middle point
            int mid = (low + high) / 2;
            // Recursively sort the first and second halves
            mergeSort(low, mid);
            mergeSort(mid + 1, high);
            // Merge the sorted halves
            merge(low, mid, high);
        }
    }
    // Method to merge two halves of the array
    private void merge(int low, int mid, int high) {
        int n1 = mid - low + 1;
        int n2 = high - mid;
        // Create temporary arrays
        int[] leftArray = new int[n1];
        int[] rightArray = new int[n2];

        // Copy data to temporary arrays
        for (int i = 0; i < n1; i++) {
```

```
            leftArray[i] = array[low + i];
        }
        for (int j = 0; j < n2; j++) {
            rightArray[j] = array[mid + 1 + j];
        }
        // Merge the temporary arrays
        // Initial indexes of the first and second subarrays
        int i = 0, j = 0;
        // Initial index of the merged subarray
        int k = low;
        while (i < n1 && j < n2) {
            if (leftArray[i] <= rightArray[j]) {
                array[k] = leftArray[i];
                i++;
            } else {
                array[k] = rightArray[j];
                j++;
            }
            k++;
        }
        // Copy remaining elements of leftArray[], if there are any
        while (i < n1) {
            array[k] = leftArray[i];
            i++;
            k++;
        }
        // Copy remaining elements of rightArray[], if there are any
        while (j < n2) {
            array[k] = rightArray[j];
            j++;
            k++;
        }
    }
```

```
    // Method to display the sorted array
    public void display() {
        System.out.print("Sorted Array: ");
        for (int value : array) {
            System.out.print(value + " ");
        }
        System.out.println();
    }
    public static void main(String[] args) {
        // Example usage
        int[] array = {64, 34, 25, 12, 22, 11, 90};
        MergeSort mergeSort = new MergeSort(array);
        // Display the original array
        System.out.print("Original Array: ");
        for (int value : array) {
            System.out.print(value + " ");
        }
        System.out.println();
        // Perform merge sort
        mergeSort.sort();
        // Display the sorted array
        mergeSort.display();
    }
}
```

In this example, the MergeSort class takes an array as a parameter in its constructor and contains methods for performing merge sort on the array. The sort method initiates the sorting process, and the merge method is a helper method that merges two halves of the array. The display method is used to print the sorted array. The main method demonstrates how to create an instance of the class, display the original array, perform the merge sort, and then display the sorted array.

You can replace the array in the main method with your own array or integrate the sort method into an existing class structure as needed.

4.5.Quick sort

Below is an example of a Java class that implements the quicksort algorithm:

```
public class QuickSort {
    private int[] array;
    public QuickSort(int[] array) {
        this.array = array;
    }
    // Method to perform quicksort on the array
    public void sort() {
        quickSort(0, array.length - 1);
    }
    // Recursive method to perform quicksort
    private void quickSort(int low, int high) {
        if (low < high) {
            // Partition the array, get the index of the pivot
            int pivotIndex = partition(low, high);
            // Recursively sort the elements before and after the pivot
            quickSort(low, pivotIndex - 1);
            quickSort(pivotIndex + 1, high);
        }
    }
    // Method to partition the array and return the index of the pivot
    private int partition(int low, int high) {
        int pivot = array[high];
        int i = low - 1;
        for (int j = low; j < high; j++) {
            if (array[j] <= pivot) {
                i++;
                // Swap array[i] and array[j]
                int temp = array[i];
                array[i] = array[j];
                array[j] = temp;
            }
```

```
        }
        // Swap array[i+1] and array[high] (pivot)
        int temp = array[i + 1];
        array[i + 1] = array[high];
        array[high] = temp;
        return i + 1;
    }
    // Method to display the sorted array
    public void display() {
        System.out.print("Sorted Array: ");
        for (int value : array) {
            System.out.print(value + " ");
        }
        System.out.println();
    }
    public static void main(String[] args) {
        // Example usage
        int[] array = {64, 34, 25, 12, 22, 11, 90};
        QuickSort quickSort = new QuickSort(array);
        // Display the original array
        System.out.print("Original Array: ");
        for (int value : array) {
            System.out.print(value + " ");
        }
        System.out.println();
        // Perform quicksort
        quickSort.sort();
        // Display the sorted array
        quickSort.display();
    }
}
```

In this example, the QuickSort class takes an array as a parameter in its constructor and contains methods for performing quicksort on the array. The sort method initiates the sorting process, the partition method is used to partition the array and find the index of the pivot, and the display method is used to print the sorted array. The main method demonstrates how to create an instance of the class, display the original array, perform the quicksort, and then display the sorted array.

You can replace the array in the main method with your own array or integrate the sort method into an existing class structure as needed.

4.6.Topological sort

Topological sorting is mainly used for scheduling tasks, and it's commonly applied to Directed Acyclic Graphs (DAGs). Here's an example of a Java class implementing topological sort:

```
import java.util.ArrayList;
import java.util.LinkedList;
import java.util.Stack;
class Graph {
    private int vertices;
    private ArrayList<LinkedList<Integer>> adjacencyList;
    public Graph(int vertices) {
        this.vertices = vertices;
        this.adjacencyList = new ArrayList<>(vertices);
        for (int i = 0; i < vertices; i++) {
            adjacencyList.add(new LinkedList<>());
        }
    }
    public void addEdge(int source, int destination) {
        adjacencyList.get(source).add(destination);
    }
    public void topologicalSort() {
        Stack<Integer> stack = new Stack<>();
        boolean[] visited = new boolean[vertices];
        for (int i = 0; i < vertices; i++) {
            if (!visited[i]) {
                topologicalSortUtil(i, visited, stack);
            }
        }
        // Print the topological order
        System.out.print("Topological Sort: ");
        while (!stack.isEmpty()) {
            System.out.print(stack.pop() + " ");
        }
```

```
        System.out.println();
    }
    private void topologicalSortUtil(int vertex, boolean[] visited, Stack<Integer> stack) {
        visited[vertex] = true;
        for (Integer neighbor : adjacencyList.get(vertex)) {
            if (!visited[neighbor]) {
                topologicalSortUtil(neighbor, visited, stack);
            }
        }
        stack.push(vertex);
    }
}
public class TopologicalSortExample {
    public static void main(String[] args) {
        // Example usage
        Graph graph = new Graph(6);
        // Adding edges to the graph
        graph.addEdge(5, 2);
        graph.addEdge(5, 0);
        graph.addEdge(4, 0);
        graph.addEdge(4, 1);
        graph.addEdge(2, 3);
        graph.addEdge(3, 1);
        // Perform topological sort
        graph.topologicalSort();
    }
}
```

In this example:

- The Graph class represents a directed graph using an adjacency list.
- The addEdge method is used to add directed edges to the graph.
- The topologicalSort method initiates the topological sorting process.
- The topologicalSortUtil method is a recursive utility function that performs the actual topological sorting.

- The main method demonstrates how to create a graph, add edges, and perform topological sorting.

You can modify the graph's edges in the main method to suit your specific use case. Note that the input graph must be a Directed Acyclic Graph (DAG) for topological sorting to be possible.

5.STACK

5.1. Implement a stack using arrays (Push and pop operations)

Below is an example of a Java class that implements a simple stack using arrays with push and pop operations:

```
public class StackUsingArray {
   private int maxSize;
   private int[] stackArray;
   private int top;
   public StackUsingArray(int size) {
      maxSize = size;
      stackArray = new int[maxSize];
      top = -1; // Initialize top to -1 when the stack is empty
   }
   // Method to push an element onto the stack
   public void push(int value) {
      if (top == maxSize - 1) {
         System.out.println("Stack overflow. Cannot push " + value);
         return;
      }
      stackArray[++top] = value;
      System.out.println(value + " pushed onto the stack");
   }
   // Method to pop an element from the stack
   public int pop() {
      if (top == -1) {
         System.out.println("Stack underflow. Cannot pop from an empty stack");
         return -1; // Return a sentinel value indicating an empty stack
      }
      int poppedValue = stackArray[top--];
      System.out.println(poppedValue + " popped from the stack");
      return poppedValue;
   }
   // Method to check if the stack is empty
```

```
    public boolean isEmpty() {
        return top == -1;
    }
    // Method to check if the stack is full
    public boolean isFull() {
        return top == maxSize - 1;
    }
    public static void main(String[] args) {
        // Example usage
        StackUsingArray stack = new StackUsingArray(5);
        // Push elements onto the stack
        stack.push(10);
        stack.push(20);
        stack.push(30);
        // Pop elements from the stack
        stack.pop();
        stack.pop();
        // Check if the stack is empty
        System.out.println("Is the stack empty? " + stack.isEmpty());
        // Push more elements onto the stack
        stack.push(40);
        stack.push(50);
        stack.push(60);
        // Pop elements until the stack is empty
        while (!stack.isEmpty()) {
            stack.pop();
        }
        // Check if the stack is full
        System.out.println("Is the stack full? " + stack.isFull());
    }
}
```

In this example:

- The StackUsingArray class represents a stack implemented using an array.

- The push method adds an element to the top of the stack.
- The pop method removes and returns the element from the top of the stack.
- The isEmpty method checks if the stack is empty.
- The isFull method checks if the stack is full.
- The main method demonstrates how to create a stack, push and pop elements, and check the stack's emptiness and fullness.

You can adjust the maxSize parameter in the constructor to change the size of the stack according to your requirements.

5.2. Implement a stack using linked lists (Push and pop operations)

Below is an example of a Java class that implements a simple stack using linked lists with push and pop operations:

```
class Node {
    int data;
    Node next;
    public Node(int data) {
        this.data = data;
        this.next = null;
    }
}
public class StackUsingLinkedList {
    private Node top;
    // Constructor to initialize an empty stack
    public StackUsingLinkedList() {
        this.top = null;
    }
    // Method to push an element onto the stack
    public void push(int value) {
        Node newNode = new Node(value);
        newNode.next = top;
        top = newNode;
        System.out.println(value + " pushed onto the stack");
    }
    // Method to pop an element from the stack
    public int pop() {
        if (isEmpty()) {
            System.out.println("Stack underflow. Cannot pop from an empty stack");
            return -1; // Return a sentinel value indicating an empty stack
        }
        int poppedValue = top.data;
        top = top.next;
        System.out.println(poppedValue + " popped from the stack");
```

```
        return poppedValue;
    }
    // Method to check if the stack is empty
    public boolean isEmpty() {
        return top == null;
    }
    public static void main(String[] args) {
        // Example usage
        StackUsingLinkedList stack = new StackUsingLinkedList();
        // Push elements onto the stack
        stack.push(10);
        stack.push(20);
        stack.push(30);
        // Pop elements from the stack
        stack.pop();
        stack.pop();
        // Check if the stack is empty
        System.out.println("Is the stack empty? " + stack.isEmpty());
        // Push more elements onto the stack
        stack.push(40);
        stack.push(50);
        stack.push(60);
        // Pop elements until the stack is empty
        while (!stack.isEmpty()) {
            stack.pop();
        }
        // Check if the stack is empty
        System.out.println("Is the stack empty? " + stack.isEmpty());
    }
}
```

In this example:

- The Node class represents a node in the linked list.
- The StackUsingLinkedList class represents a stack implemented using a linked list.

- The push method adds a new node with the given value to the top of the stack.
- The pop method removes and returns the node from the top of the stack.
- The isEmpty method checks if the stack is empty.
- The main method demonstrates how to create a stack, push and pop elements, and check the stack's emptiness.

You can adapt this implementation based on your specific needs or integrate it into your existing class structure.

5.3. Evaluate a post fix expression using a stack

Below is an example of a Java class that evaluates a postfix expression using a stack:

```
import java.util.Stack;
public class PostfixExpressionEvaluator {
  // Method to evaluate a postfix expression
  public static int evaluatePostfix(String expression) {
    Stack<Integer> stack = new Stack<>();
    for (char c : expression.toCharArray()) {
      if (Character.isDigit(c)) {
        stack.push(Character.getNumericValue(c));
      } else {
        int operand2 = stack.pop();
        int operand1 = stack.pop();
        int result = performOperation(c, operand1, operand2);
        stack.push(result);
      }
    }
    return stack.pop();
  }
  // Method to perform an operation based on the operator
  private static int performOperation(char operator, int operand1, int operand2) {
    switch (operator) {
      case '+':
        return operand1 + operand2;
      case '-':
        return operand1 - operand2;
      case '*':
        return operand1 * operand2;
      case '/':
        if (operand2 != 0) {
          return operand1 / operand2;
        } else {
          throw new ArithmeticException("Cannot divide by zero");
```

```
            }
        default:
            throw new IllegalArgumentException("Invalid operator: " + operator);
        }
    }
    public static void main(String[] args) {
        // Example usage
        String postfixExpression = "23*5+";
        int result = evaluatePostfix(postfixExpression);
        System.out.println("Postfix Expression: " + postfixExpression);
        System.out.println("Result: " + result);
    }
}
```

In this example:

- The evaluatePostfix method takes a postfix expression as a string and uses a stack to evaluate the expression.
- The performOperation method is a helper method that performs basic arithmetic operations based on the operator.
- The main method demonstrates how to use the class by providing a postfix expression and obtaining the result.

You can replace the postfixExpression variable in the main method with your own postfix expression to test the evaluation. Make sure that the expression is well-formed and adheres to the postfix notation rules.

5.4. Use a stack to check for balanced parentheses in an expression

Below is an example of a Java class that uses a stack to check for balanced parentheses in an expression:

```
import java.util.Stack;
public class BalancedParenthesesChecker {
    // Method to check for balanced parentheses in an expression
    public static boolean areParenthesesBalanced(String expression) {
        Stack<Character> stack = new Stack<>();
        for (char c : expression.toCharArray()) {
            if (isOpeningParenthesis(c)) {
                stack.push(c);
            } else if (isClosingParenthesis(c)) {
                if (stack.isEmpty() || !isMatchingPair(stack.pop(), c)) {
                    return false;
                }
            }
        }
        return stack.isEmpty();
    }
    // Method to check if a character is an opening parenthesis
    private static boolean isOpeningParenthesis(char c) {
        return c == '(' || c == '[' || c == '{';
    }
    // Method to check if a character is a closing parenthesis
    private static boolean isClosingParenthesis(char c) {
        return c == ')' || c == ']' || c == '}';
    }
    // Method to check if two parentheses form a matching pair
    private static boolean isMatchingPair(char opening, char closing) {
        return (opening == '(' && closing == ')') ||
                (opening == '[' && closing == ']') ||
                (opening == '{' && closing == '}');
    }
```

```
    public static void main(String[] args) {
        // Example usage
        String expression1 = "{[()]}";
        String expression2 = "{[(])}";
        System.out.println("Expression: " + expression1);
        System.out.println("Balanced: " + areParenthesesBalanced(expression1));
        System.out.println("Expression: " + expression2);
        System.out.println("Balanced: " + areParenthesesBalanced(expression2));
    }
}
```

In this example:

- The areParenthesesBalanced method takes an expression as a string and uses a stack to check if the parentheses in the expression are balanced.
- The isOpeningParenthesis, isClosingParenthesis, and isMatchingPair methods are helper methods to determine the type of a parenthesis and whether two parentheses form a matching pair.
- The main method demonstrates how to use the class by providing two expressions and checking if their parentheses are balanced.

You can replace the expression1 and expression2 variables in the main method with your own expressions to test the balanced parentheses checker.

6.QUEUE

6.1. Implement a queue using arrays (enqueue and dequeue operations)

Below is an example of a Java class that implements a simple queue using arrays with enqueue and dequeue operations:

```
public class QueueUsingArray {
    private int maxSize;
    private int[] queueArray;
    private int front;
    private int rear;
    private int size;
    public QueueUsingArray(int size) {
        this.maxSize = size;
        this.queueArray = new int[maxSize];
        this.front = 0;
        this.rear = -1;
        this.size = 0;
    }
    // Method to enqueue (insert) an element into the queue
    public void enqueue(int value) {
        if (isFull()) {
            System.out.println("Queue overflow. Cannot enqueue " + value);
            return;
        }
        rear = (rear + 1) % maxSize;
        queueArray[rear] = value;
        size++;
        System.out.println(value + " enqueued into the queue");
    }
    // Method to dequeue (remove) an element from the queue
    public int dequeue() {
        if (isEmpty()) {
            System.out.println("Queue underflow. Cannot dequeue from an empty queue");
            return -1; // Return a sentinel value indicating an empty queue
```

```
        }
        int dequeuedValue = queueArray[front];
        front = (front + 1) % maxSize;
        size--;
        System.out.println(dequeuedValue + " dequeued from the queue");
        return dequeuedValue;
    }
    // Method to check if the queue is empty
    public boolean isEmpty() {
        return size == 0;
    }
    // Method to check if the queue is full
    public boolean isFull() {
        return size == maxSize;
    }
    public static void main(String[] args) {
        // Example usage
        QueueUsingArray queue = new QueueUsingArray(5);
        // Enqueue elements into the queue
        queue.enqueue(10);
        queue.enqueue(20);
        queue.enqueue(30);
        // Dequeue elements from the queue
        queue.dequeue();
        queue.dequeue();
        // Check if the queue is empty
        System.out.println("Is the queue empty? " + queue.isEmpty());
        // Enqueue more elements into the queue
        queue.enqueue(40);
        queue.enqueue(50);
        queue.enqueue(60);
        // Dequeue elements until the queue is empty
        while (!queue.isEmpty()) {
```

```
            queue.dequeue();
        }
        // Check if the queue is full
        System.out.println("Is the queue full? " + queue.isFull());
    }
}
```

In this example:

- The QueueUsingArray class represents a queue implemented using an array.
- The enqueue method adds an element to the rear of the queue.
- The dequeue method removes and returns the element from the front of the queue.
- The isEmpty method checks if the queue is empty.
- The isFull method checks if the queue is full.
- The main method demonstrates how to create a queue, enqueue and dequeue elements, and check the queue's emptiness and fullness.

You can adjust the maxSize parameter in the constructor to change the size of the queue according to your requirements.

6.2. Implement a queue using linked lists (enqueue and dequeue operations)

Below is an example of a Java class that implements a simple queue using linked lists with enqueue and dequeue operations:

```
class Node {
    int data;
    Node next;
    public Node(int data) {
        this.data = data;
        this.next = null;
    }
}
public class QueueUsingLinkedList {
    private Node front;
    private Node rear;
    // Constructor to initialize an empty queue
    public QueueUsingLinkedList() {
        this.front = null;
        this.rear = null;
    }
    // Method to enqueue (insert) an element into the queue
    public void enqueue(int value) {
        Node newNode = new Node(value);
        if (isEmpty()) {
            front = rear = newNode;
        } else {
            rear.next = newNode;
            rear = newNode;
        }
        System.out.println(value + " enqueued into the queue");
    }
    // Method to dequeue (remove) an element from the queue
    public int dequeue() {
        if (isEmpty()) {
```

```
            System.out.println("Queue underflow. Cannot dequeue from an empty queue");
            return -1; // Return a sentinel value indicating an empty queue
        }
        int dequeuedValue = front.data;
        if (front == rear) {
            // If there is only one element in the queue
            front = rear = null;
        } else {
            front = front.next;
        }
        System.out.println(dequeuedValue + " dequeued from the queue");
        return dequeuedValue;
    }
    // Method to check if the queue is empty
    public boolean isEmpty() {
        return front == null;
    }
    public static void main(String[] args) {
        // Example usage
        QueueUsingLinkedList queue = new QueueUsingLinkedList();
        // Enqueue elements into the queue
        queue.enqueue(10);
        queue.enqueue(20);
        queue.enqueue(30);
        // Dequeue elements from the queue
        queue.dequeue();
        queue.dequeue();
        // Check if the queue is empty
        System.out.println("Is the queue empty? " + queue.isEmpty());
        // Enqueue more elements into the queue
        queue.enqueue(40);
        queue.enqueue(50);
        queue.enqueue(60);
```

```
        // Dequeue elements until the queue is empty
        while (!queue.isEmpty()) {
            queue.dequeue();
        }
        // Check if the queue is empty
        System.out.println("Is the queue empty? " + queue.isEmpty());
    }
}
```

In this example:

- The Node class represents a node in the linked list.
- The QueueUsingLinkedList class represents a queue implemented using a linked list.
- The enqueue method adds a new node with the given value to the rear of the queue.
- The dequeue method removes and returns the node from the front of the queue.
- The isEmpty method checks if the queue is empty.
- The main method demonstrates how to use the class by providing a queue, enqueue and dequeue elements, and check the queue's emptiness.

You can adapt this implementation based on your specific needs or integrate it into your existing class structure.

6.3. Circular queue implementation (enqueue and dequeue operations)

Below is an example of a Java class that implements a circular queue using arrays with enqueue and dequeue operations:

```
public class CircularQueue {
    private int maxSize;
    private int[] queueArray;
    private int front;
    private int rear;
    public CircularQueue(int size) {
        this.maxSize = size;
        this.queueArray = new int[maxSize];
        this.front = -1;
        this.rear = -1;
    }
    // Method to enqueue (insert) an element into the circular queue
    public void enqueue(int value) {
        if (isFull()) {
            System.out.println("Queue overflow. Cannot enqueue " + value);
            return;
        }
        if (isEmpty()) {
            front = rear = 0;
        } else {
            rear = (rear + 1) % maxSize;
        }
        queueArray[rear] = value;
        System.out.println(value + " enqueued into the circular queue");
    }
    // Method to dequeue (remove) an element from the circular queue
    public int dequeue() {
        if (isEmpty()) {
            System.out.println("Queue underflow. Cannot dequeue from an empty queue");
            return -1; // Return a sentinel value indicating an empty queue
```

```
        }
        int dequeuedValue = queueArray[front];
        if (front == rear) {
            // If there is only one element in the queue
            front = rear = -1;
        } else {
            front = (front + 1) % maxSize;
        }
        System.out.println(dequeuedValue + " dequeued from the circular queue");
        return dequeuedValue;
    }
    // Method to check if the circular queue is empty
    public boolean isEmpty() {
        return front == -1 && rear == -1;
    }
    // Method to check if the circular queue is full
    public boolean isFull() {
        return (rear + 1) % maxSize == front;
    }
    public static void main(String[] args) {
        // Example usage
        CircularQueue circularQueue = new CircularQueue(5);
        // Enqueue elements into the circular queue
        circularQueue.enqueue(10);
        circularQueue.enqueue(20);
        circularQueue.enqueue(30);
        // Dequeue elements from the circular queue
        circularQueue.dequeue();
        circularQueue.dequeue();
        // Check if the circular queue is empty
        System.out.println("Is the circular queue empty? " + circularQueue.isEmpty());
        // Enqueue more elements into the circular queue
        circularQueue.enqueue(40);
```

```
        circularQueue.enqueue(50);
        circularQueue.enqueue(60);
        // Dequeue elements until the circular queue is empty
        while (!circularQueue.isEmpty()) {
            circularQueue.dequeue();
        }
        // Check if the circular queue is full
        System.out.println("Is the circular queue full? " + circularQueue.isFull());
    }
}
```

In this example:

- The CircularQueue class represents a circular queue implemented using an array.
- The enqueue method adds an element to the rear of the circular queue.
- The dequeue method removes and returns the element from the front of the circular queue.
- The isEmpty method checks if the circular queue is empty.
- The isFull method checks if the circular queue is full.
- The main method demonstrates how to create a circular queue, enqueue and dequeue elements, and check the circular queue's emptiness and fullness.

You can adjust the maxSize parameter in the constructor to change the size of the circular queue according to your requirements.

6.4. Simulate a real-world scenario using a queue (Ex. Print queue)

Let's simulate a print queue as a real-world scenario using a Java class. In a print queue, print jobs are added to the queue and processed in a first-come, first-served manner.

```
import java.util.LinkedList;
import java.util.Queue;
class PrintJob {
   private String document;
   public PrintJob(String document) {
      this.document = document;
   }
   public String getDocument() {
      return document;
   }
}
class PrintQueue {
   private Queue<PrintJob> jobQueue;
   public PrintQueue() {
      this.jobQueue = new LinkedList<>();
   }
   // Enqueue (add) a print job to the print queue
   public void enqueue(PrintJob job) {
      jobQueue.offer(job);
      System.out.println("Print job enqueued: " + job.getDocument());
   }
   // Dequeue (process) a print job from the print queue
   public PrintJob dequeue() {
      PrintJob job = jobQueue.poll();
      if (job != null) {
         System.out.println("Printing: " + job.getDocument());
      } else {
         System.out.println("Print queue is empty. No job to print.");
      }
      return job;
```

```
    }
    // Check if the print queue is empty
    public boolean isEmpty() {
        return jobQueue.isEmpty();
    }
}
public class PrintQueueSimulation {
    public static void main(String[] args) {
        // Example usage
        PrintQueue printQueue = new PrintQueue();
        // Enqueue print jobs
        printQueue.enqueue(new PrintJob("Document1"));
        printQueue.enqueue(new PrintJob("Document2"));
        printQueue.enqueue(new PrintJob("Document3"));
        // Process print jobs until the queue is empty
        while (!printQueue.isEmpty()) {
            printQueue.dequeue();
        }
    }
}
```

In this example:

- The PrintJob class represents a print job with a document to be printed.
- The PrintQueue class represents the print queue, which is implemented using a Queue (in this case, a LinkedList).
- The enqueue method adds a print job to the print queue.
- The dequeue method processes the next print job in the queue (prints it).
- The isEmpty method checks if the print queue is empty.
- The PrintQueueSimulation class demonstrates how to use the print queue by enqueuing print jobs and processing them.

7. TREE

7.1. Binary tree traversal (In-order, Pre-order and Post-order)

Below is an example of a Java class that represents a binary tree and performs in-order, pre-order, and post-order traversals:

```
class TreeNode {
    int data;
    TreeNode left;
    TreeNode right;
    public TreeNode(int data) {
        this.data = data;
        this.left = null;
        this.right = null;
    }
}
public class BinaryTreeTraversal {
    private TreeNode root;
    public BinaryTreeTraversal() {
        this.root = null;
    }
    // Method to perform in-order traversal
    public void inOrderTraversal(TreeNode node) {
        if (node != null) {
            inOrderTraversal(node.left);
            System.out.print(node.data + " ");
            inOrderTraversal(node.right);
        }
    }
    // Method to perform pre-order traversal
    public void preOrderTraversal(TreeNode node) {
        if (node != null) {
            System.out.print(node.data + " ");
            preOrderTraversal(node.left);
            preOrderTraversal(node.right);
```

```
        }
    }
    // Method to perform post-order traversal
    public void postOrderTraversal(TreeNode node) {
        if (node != null) {
            postOrderTraversal(node.left);
            postOrderTraversal(node.right);
            System.out.print(node.data + " ");
        }
    }
    public static void main(String[] args) {
        // Example usage
        BinaryTreeTraversal binaryTree = new BinaryTreeTraversal();
        // Create a sample binary tree
        binaryTree.root = new TreeNode(1);
        binaryTree.root.left = new TreeNode(2);
        binaryTree.root.right = new TreeNode(3);
        binaryTree.root.left.left = new TreeNode(4);
        binaryTree.root.left.right = new TreeNode(5);
        // Perform in-order traversal
        System.out.println("In-order traversal:");
        binaryTree.inOrderTraversal(binaryTree.root);
        System.out.println();
        // Perform pre-order traversal
        System.out.println("Pre-order traversal:");
        binaryTree.preOrderTraversal(binaryTree.root);
        System.out.println();
        // Perform post-order traversal
        System.out.println("Post-order traversal:");
        binaryTree.postOrderTraversal(binaryTree.root);
        System.out.println();
    }
}
```

In this example:

- The TreeNode class represents a node in the binary tree.
- The BinaryTreeTraversal class represents the binary tree and contains methods for in-order, pre-order, and post-order traversals.
- The inOrderTraversal, preOrderTraversal, and postOrderTraversal methods are recursive methods that perform the respective traversals.
- The main method demonstrates how to create a binary tree and perform in-order, pre-order, and post-order traversals.

You can customize the binary tree structure and add more nodes to see how the different traversal methods work.

7.2. Find the height of a binary tree.

Below is an example of a Java class that represents a binary tree and calculates its height:

```
class TreeNode {
    int data;
    TreeNode left;
    TreeNode right;
    public TreeNode(int data) {
        this.data = data;
        this.left = null;
        this.right = null;
    }
}
public class BinaryTreeHeight {
    private TreeNode root;
    public BinaryTreeHeight() {
        this.root = null;
    }
    // Method to calculate the height of the binary tree
    public int calculateHeight(TreeNode node) {
        if (node == null) {
            return 0;
        } else {
            int leftSubtreeHeight = calculateHeight(node.left);
            int rightSubtreeHeight = calculateHeight(node.right);
            // Return the maximum of the left and right subtree heights plus 1
            return Math.max(leftSubtreeHeight, rightSubtreeHeight) + 1;
        }
    }
    public static void main(String[] args) {
        // Example usage
        BinaryTreeHeight binaryTree = new BinaryTreeHeight();
        // Create a sample binary tree
```

```
        binaryTree.root = new TreeNode(1);
        binaryTree.root.left = new TreeNode(2);
        binaryTree.root.right = new TreeNode(3);
        binaryTree.root.left.left = new TreeNode(4);
        binaryTree.root.left.right = new TreeNode(5);
        // Calculate the height of the binary tree
        int height = binaryTree.calculateHeight(binaryTree.root);
        System.out.println("Height of the binary tree: " + height);
    }
}
```

In this example:

- The TreeNode class represents a node in the binary tree.
- The BinaryTreeHeight class represents the binary tree and contains a method calculateHeight to recursively calculate the height.
- The calculateHeight method calculates the height of the binary tree using a recursive approach, finding the maximum height between the left and right subtrees and adding 1.

You can customize the binary tree structure by adding more nodes to see how the height calculation works for different tree shapes.

7.3. Binary Search tree insert, delete, display and search operations

Below is an example of a Java class that represents a Binary Search Tree (BST) and includes methods for insert, delete, display, and search operations:

```
class TreeNode {
   int key;
   TreeNode left, right;
   public TreeNode(int key) {
      this.key = key;
      this.left = this.right = null;
   }
}
public class BinarySearchTree {
   private TreeNode root;
   public BinarySearchTree() {
      this.root = null;
   }
   // Method to insert a key into the BST
   public void insert(int key) {
      root = insertRecursive(root, key);
   }
   private TreeNode insertRecursive(TreeNode root, int key) {
      if (root == null) {
         return new TreeNode(key);
      }
      if (key < root.key) {
         root.left = insertRecursive(root.left, key);
      } else if (key > root.key) {
         root.right = insertRecursive(root.right, key);
      }
      return root;
   }
   // Method to delete a key from the BST
   public void delete(int key) {
```

```
    root = deleteRecursive(root, key);
  }
  private TreeNode deleteRecursive(TreeNode root, int key) {
    if (root == null) {
      return root;
    }
    if (key < root.key) {
      root.left = deleteRecursive(root.left, key);
    } else if (key > root.key) {
      root.right = deleteRecursive(root.right, key);
    } else {
      // Node with only one child or no child
      if (root.left == null) {
        return root.right;
      } else if (root.right == null) {
        return root.left;
      }
      // Node with two children
      root.key = minValue(root.right);
      // Delete the in-order successor
      root.right = deleteRecursive(root.right, root.key);
    }
    return root;
  }
  private int minValue(TreeNode root) {
    int minValue = root.key;
    while (root.left != null) {
      minValue = root.left.key;
      root = root.left;
    }
    return minValue;
  }
  // Method to search for a key in the BST
```

```
public boolean search(int key) {
    return searchRecursive(root, key);
}
private boolean searchRecursive(TreeNode root, int key) {
    if (root == null || root.key == key) {
        return root != null;
    }
    if (key < root.key) {
        return searchRecursive(root.left, key);
    } else {
        return searchRecursive(root.right, key);
    }
}
// Method to display the BST in-order
public void displayInOrder() {
    displayInOrderRecursive(root);
    System.out.println();
}
private void displayInOrderRecursive(TreeNode root) {
    if (root != null) {
        displayInOrderRecursive(root.left);
        System.out.print(root.key + " ");
        displayInOrderRecursive(root.right);
    }
}
public static void main(String[] args) {
    // Example usage
    BinarySearchTree bst = new BinarySearchTree();
    bst.insert(50);
    bst.insert(30);
    bst.insert(70);
    bst.insert(20);
    bst.insert(40);
```

```
        bst.insert(60);
        bst.insert(80);
        System.out.println("In-order traversal:");
        bst.displayInOrder();
        int keyToDelete = 30;
        System.out.println("Deleting key " + keyToDelete);
        bst.delete(keyToDelete);
        bst.displayInOrder();
        int keyToSearch = 60;
        System.out.println("Searching for key " + keyToSearch + ": " +
bst.search(keyToSearch));
    }
}
```

In this example:

- The TreeNode class represents a node in the binary search tree.
- The BinarySearchTree class contains methods for insert, delete, search, and display (in-order traversal) operations.
- The insertRecursive, deleteRecursive, searchRecursive, and displayInOrderRecursive methods are recursive implementations of the respective operations.
- The main method demonstrates example usage by creating a BST, inserting nodes, deleting a node, searching for a node, and displaying the tree.

7.4.AVL tree (or) Red-black tree implementation

Implementing a balanced binary search tree like AVL tree or Red-Black tree requires a more complex structure and several algorithms to maintain balance during insertion and deletion operations. Below is a simple implementation of an AVL tree in Java. Note that the Red-Black tree implementation would be more complex.

```
class AVLNode {
    int key, height;
    AVLNode left, right;
    public AVLNode(int key) {
        this.key = key;
        this.height = 1;
        this.left = this.right = null;
    }
}
public class AVLTree {
    private AVLNode root;
    public AVLTree() {
        this.root = null;
    }
    // Get the height of a node
    private int height(AVLNode node) {
        if (node == null) {
            return 0;
        }
        return node.height;
    }
    // Get the balance factor of a node
    private int getBalance(AVLNode node) {
        if (node == null) {
            return 0;
        }
        return height(node.left) - height(node.right);
    }
```

```
// Rotate right sub-tree rooted with y
private AVLNode rightRotate(AVLNode y) {
    AVLNode x = y.left;
    AVLNode T2 = x.right;
    // Perform rotation
    x.right = y;
    y.left = T2;
    // Update heights
    y.height = Math.max(height(y.left), height(y.right)) + 1;
    x.height = Math.max(height(x.left), height(x.right)) + 1;
    return x;
}
// Rotate left sub-tree rooted with x
private AVLNode leftRotate(AVLNode x) {
    AVLNode y = x.right;
    AVLNode T2 = y.left;
    // Perform rotation
    y.left = x;
    x.right = T2;
    // Update heights
    x.height = Math.max(height(x.left), height(x.right)) + 1;
    y.height = Math.max(height(y.left), height(y.right)) + 1;
    return y;
}
// Insert a key into the AVL tree
public void insert(int key) {
    root = insertRecursive(root, key);
}
private AVLNode insertRecursive(AVLNode node, int key) {
    // Perform standard BST insertion
    if (node == null) {
        return new AVLNode(key);
    }
```

```
        if (key < node.key) {
            node.left = insertRecursive(node.left, key);
        } else if (key > node.key) {
            node.right = insertRecursive(node.right, key);
        } else {
            // Duplicate keys are not allowed in AVL tree
            return node;
        }
        // Update height of current node
        node.height = 1 + Math.max(height(node.left), height(node.right));
        // Get the balance factor to check whether this node became unbalanced
        int balance = getBalance(node);
        // Left-Left Case (LL)
        if (balance > 1 && key < node.left.key) {
            return rightRotate(node);
        }
        // Right-Right Case (RR)
        if (balance < -1 && key > node.right.key) {
            return leftRotate(node);
        }
        // Left-Right Case (LR)
        if (balance > 1 && key > node.left.key) {
            node.left = leftRotate(node.left);
            return rightRotate(node);
        }
        // Right-Left Case (RL)
        if (balance < -1 && key < node.right.key) {
            node.right = rightRotate(node.right);
            return leftRotate(node);
        }
        return node;
    }
    // Perform in-order traversal of the AVL tree
```

```
    public void inOrderTraversal() {
        inOrderTraversalRecursive(root);
        System.out.println();
    }
    private void inOrderTraversalRecursive(AVLNode node) {
        if (node != null) {
            inOrderTraversalRecursive(node.left);
            System.out.print(node.key + " ");
            inOrderTraversalRecursive(node.right);
        }
    }
    public static void main(String[] args) {
        // Example usage
        AVLTree avlTree = new AVLTree();
        avlTree.insert(10);
        avlTree.insert(20);
        avlTree.insert(30);
        avlTree.insert(40);
        avlTree.insert(50);
        avlTree.insert(25);
        System.out.println("In-order traversal after insertion:");
        avlTree.inOrderTraversal();
    }
}
```

In this example:

- The AVLNode class represents a node in the AVL tree.
- The AVLTree class contains methods for insertion and in-order traversal.
- The rightRotate, leftRotate, getBalance, and height methods are helper methods for AVL tree balancing.
- The insertRecursive method performs the standard BST insertion and then checks for AVL tree balance conditions.
- The inOrderTraversal and inOrderTraversalRecursive methods perform in-order traversal to display the elements of the AVL tree.

This is a basic example, and for a complete and production-ready AVL tree implementation, you may need to add more features and handle additional cases for deletion and rebalancing.

7.5. Check if a binary tree is balanced

To check if a binary tree is balanced, you need to ensure that the height difference between the left and right subtrees of every node is at most 1. Below is an example of a Java class that checks if a binary tree is balanced:

```
class TreeNode {
    int key;
    TreeNode left, right;
    public TreeNode(int key) {
        this.key = key;
        this.left = null;
        this.right = null;
    }
}
public class BalancedBinaryTree {
    private TreeNode root;
    public BalancedBinaryTree() {
        this.root = null;
    }
    // Method to check if the binary tree is balanced
    public boolean isBalanced() {
        return isBalancedRecursive(root);
    }
    private boolean isBalancedRecursive(TreeNode node) {
        if (node == null) {
            return true;
        }
        int leftHeight = getHeight(node.left);
        int rightHeight = getHeight(node.right);
        // Check if the current node is balanced
        if (Math.abs(leftHeight - rightHeight) <= 1 &&
            isBalancedRecursive(node.left) &&
            isBalancedRecursive(node.right)) {
            return true;
```

```
        }
        return false;
    }
    // Method to calculate the height of a node
    private int getHeight(TreeNode node) {
        if (node == null) {
            return 0;
        }
        int leftHeight = getHeight(node.left);
        int rightHeight = getHeight(node.right);
        return Math.max(leftHeight, rightHeight) + 1;
    }
    public static void main(String[] args) {
        // Example usage
        BalancedBinaryTree binaryTree = new BalancedBinaryTree();
        binaryTree.root = new TreeNode(1);
        binaryTree.root.left = new TreeNode(2);
        binaryTree.root.right = new TreeNode(3);
        binaryTree.root.left.left = new TreeNode(4);
        binaryTree.root.left.right = new TreeNode(5);
        boolean isBalanced = binaryTree.isBalanced();
        System.out.println("Is the binary tree balanced? " + isBalanced);
    }
}
```

In this example:

- The TreeNode class represents a node in the binary tree.
- The BalancedBinaryTree class contains methods for checking if the binary tree is balanced.
- The isBalanced method is the public method that checks if the binary tree is balanced. It calls the private recursive method isBalancedRecursive to perform the check.
- The getHeight method calculates the height of a node.

You can customize the binary tree structure by adding more nodes and test the isBalanced method to check if the tree remains balanced.

7.6.Convert a binary search tree to a doubly linked list

To convert a Binary Search Tree (BST) to a doubly linked list, you can perform an in-order traversal of the tree while updating the pointers to create the doubly linked list. Here's an example implementation in Java:

```
class TreeNode {
    int key;
    TreeNode left, right;
    public TreeNode(int key) {
        this.key = key;
        this.left = this.right = null;
    }
}
class DoublyLinkedListNode {
    int key;
    DoublyLinkedListNode prev, next;
    public DoublyLinkedListNode(int key) {
        this.key = key;
        this.prev = this.next = null;
    }
}
public class BSTToDoublyLinkedList {
    private TreeNode root;
    private DoublyLinkedListNode head, tail;
    public BSTToDoublyLinkedList() {
        this.root = null;
        this.head = this.tail = null;
    }
    // Convert BST to doubly linked list
    public DoublyLinkedListNode convertToDoublyLinkedList(TreeNode root) {
        if (root == null) {
            return null;
        }
        // Recursively convert the left subtree
```

```
        convertToDoublyLinkedList(root.left);
        // Create a doubly linked list node for the current root
        DoublyLinkedListNode newNode = new DoublyLinkedListNode(root.key);
        // If the linked list is empty, set the head and tail to the current node
        if (head == null) {
            head = tail = newNode;
        } else {
            // Otherwise, update the next and previous pointers
            tail.next = newNode;
            newNode.prev = tail;
            tail = newNode;
        }
        // Recursively convert the right subtree
        convertToDoublyLinkedList(root.right);
        return head;
    }
    // Display the doubly linked list
    public void displayDoublyLinkedList(DoublyLinkedListNode head) {
        System.out.println("Doubly Linked List:");
        DoublyLinkedListNode current = head;
        while (current != null) {
            System.out.print(current.key + " ");
            current = current.next;
        }
        System.out.println();
    }
    public static void main(String[] args) {
        // Example usage
        BSTToDoublyLinkedList bstToDoublyLinkedList = new BSTToDoublyLinkedList();

        // Construct a sample BST
        bstToDoublyLinkedList.root = new TreeNode(4);
        bstToDoublyLinkedList.root.left = new TreeNode(2);
```

```
        bstToDoublyLinkedList.root.right = new TreeNode(5);
        bstToDoublyLinkedList.root.left.left = new TreeNode(1);
        bstToDoublyLinkedList.root.left.right = new TreeNode(3);
        // Convert BST to doubly linked list
        DoublyLinkedListNode head =
bstToDoublyLinkedList.convertToDoublyLinkedList(bstToDoublyLinkedList.root);
        // Display the doubly linked list
        bstToDoublyLinkedList.displayDoublyLinkedList(head);
    }
}
```

In this example:

- The TreeNode class represents a node in the binary search tree.
- The DoublyLinkedListNode class represents a node in the doubly linked list.
- The BSTToDoublyLinkedList class contains methods to convert a BST to a doubly linked list and display the doubly linked list.
- The convertToDoublyLinkedList method recursively converts the BST to a doubly linked list in in-order traversal.
- The displayDoublyLinkedList method displays the nodes of the doubly linked list.

You can customize the BST structure by adding more nodes and test the convertToDoublyLinkedList method to see the resulting doubly linked list.

8.GRAPHS

8.1. Implement an adjacency matrix

Below is an example of a Java class that implements an adjacency matrix for a graph:

```
class Graph {
    private int vertices;
    private boolean[][] adjacencyMatrix;
    public Graph(int vertices) {
        this.vertices = vertices;
        this.adjacencyMatrix = new boolean[vertices][vertices];
    }
    // Add an edge to the graph
    public void addEdge(int source, int destination) {
        if (source >= 0 && source < vertices && destination >= 0 && destination < vertices) {
            adjacencyMatrix[source][destination] = true;
            adjacencyMatrix[destination][source] = true;
        } else {
            System.out.println("Invalid vertices");
        }
    }
    // Display the adjacency matrix
    public void displayAdjacencyMatrix() {
        System.out.println("Adjacency Matrix:");
        for (int i = 0; i < vertices; i++) {
            for (int j = 0; j < vertices; j++) {
                System.out.print(adjacencyMatrix[i][j] ? "1 " : "0 ");
            }
            System.out.println();
        }
    }
}
```

```
public class AdjacencyMatrixExample {
    public static void main(String[] args) {
        // Example usage
        int numberOfVertices = 5;
        Graph graph = new Graph(numberOfVertices);
        // Add edges to the graph
        graph.addEdge(0, 1);
        graph.addEdge(0, 4);
        graph.addEdge(1, 2);
        graph.addEdge(1, 3);
        graph.addEdge(1, 4);
        graph.addEdge(2, 3);
        graph.addEdge(3, 4);
        // Display the adjacency matrix
        graph.displayAdjacencyMatrix();
    }
}
```

In this example:

- The Graph class represents an undirected graph using an adjacency matrix.
- The adjacencyMatrix is a 2D boolean array where adjacencyMatrix[i][j] is true if there is an edge between vertices i and j, and false otherwise.
- The addEdge method adds an edge between two vertices by setting the corresponding entries in the adjacency matrix to true.
- The displayAdjacencyMatrix method displays the adjacency matrix.

You can customize the number of vertices and edges in the graph by modifying the numberOfVertices variable and calling the addEdge method with appropriate vertex indices.

8.2. Implement an adjacency list

Below is an example of a Java class that implements an adjacency list for an undirected graph using an array of linked lists:

```
import java.util.LinkedList;
class Graph {
    private int vertices;
    private LinkedList<Integer>[] adjacencyList;
    public Graph(int vertices) {
        this.vertices = vertices;
        this.adjacencyList = new LinkedList[vertices];
        for (int i = 0; i < vertices; i++) {
            adjacencyList[i] = new LinkedList<>();
        }
    }
    // Add an edge to the graph
    public void addEdge(int source, int destination) {
        if (source >= 0 && source < vertices && destination >= 0 && destination < vertices) {
            adjacencyList[source].add(destination);
            adjacencyList[destination].add(source);
        } else {
            System.out.println("Invalid vertices");
        }
    }
    // Display the adjacency list
    public void displayAdjacencyList() {
        System.out.println("Adjacency List:");
        for (int i = 0; i < vertices; i++) {
            System.out.print(i + ": ");
            for (Integer neighbor : adjacencyList[i]) {
                System.out.print(neighbor + " ");
            }
            System.out.println();
        }
```

```
    }
}
public class AdjacencyListExample {
    public static void main(String[] args) {
        // Example usage
        int numberOfVertices = 5;
        Graph graph = new Graph(numberOfVertices);
        // Add edges to the graph
        graph.addEdge(0, 1);
        graph.addEdge(0, 4);
        graph.addEdge(1, 2);
        graph.addEdge(1, 3);
        graph.addEdge(1, 4);
        graph.addEdge(2, 3);
        graph.addEdge(3, 4);
        // Display the adjacency list
        graph.displayAdjacencyList();
    }
}
```

In this example:

- The Graph class represents an undirected graph using an adjacency list.
- The adjacencyList is an array of linked lists, where adjacencyList[i] represents the list of neighbors for vertex i.
- The addEdge method adds an edge between two vertices by adding each vertex to the other's adjacency list.
- The displayAdjacencyList method displays the adjacency list.

You can customize the number of vertices and edges in the graph by modifying the numberOfVertices variable and calling the addEdge method with appropriate vertex indices.

8.3.DFS

Below is an example of Depth-First Search (DFS) implemented in Java using a class for a graph represented by an adjacency list:

```
import java.util.LinkedList;
import java.util.Stack;

class Graph {
    private int vertices;
    private LinkedList<Integer>[] adjacencyList;

    public Graph(int vertices) {
        this.vertices = vertices;
        this.adjacencyList = new LinkedList[vertices];

        for (int i = 0; i < vertices; i++) {
            adjacencyList[i] = new LinkedList<>();
        }
    }

    // Add an edge to the graph
    public void addEdge(int source, int destination) {
        if (source >= 0 && source < vertices && destination >= 0 && destination < vertices) {
            adjacencyList[source].add(destination);
        } else {
            System.out.println("Invalid vertices");
        }
    }

    // Perform DFS traversal starting from a given vertex
    public void DFS(int startVertex) {
        boolean[] visited = new boolean[vertices];
```

```
        // Create a stack for DFS
        Stack<Integer> stack = new Stack<>();

        // Push the current source node
        stack.push(startVertex);

        while (!stack.isEmpty()) {
            // Pop a vertex from the stack and print it
            int currentVertex = stack.pop();

            if (!visited[currentVertex]) {
                System.out.print(currentVertex + " ");
                visited[currentVertex] = true;
            }

            // Get all adjacent vertices of the popped vertex
            // If an adjacent vertex is not visited, push it to the stack
            for (int neighbor : adjacencyList[currentVertex]) {
                if (!visited[neighbor]) {
                    stack.push(neighbor);
                }
            }
        }
    }
}

public class DFSExample {
    public static void main(String[] args) {
        // Example usage
        int numberOfVertices = 7;
        Graph graph = new Graph(numberOfVertices);

        // Add edges to the graph
```

```
        graph.addEdge(0, 1);
        graph.addEdge(0, 2);
        graph.addEdge(1, 3);
        graph.addEdge(1, 4);
        graph.addEdge(2, 5);
        graph.addEdge(2, 6);

        // Perform DFS starting from vertex 0
        System.out.println("DFS traversal starting from vertex 0:");
        graph.DFS(0);
    }
}
```

In this example:

- The Graph class represents an undirected graph using an adjacency list.
- The DFS method performs Depth-First Search starting from a given vertex. It uses a stack to keep track of vertices to visit.
- The addEdge method adds an edge between two vertices by adding the destination vertex to the source vertex's adjacency list.
- The main method demonstrates example usage by creating a graph, adding edges, and performing DFS starting from vertex 0.

You can customize the number of vertices and edges in the graph by modifying the numberOfVertices variable and calling the addEdge method with appropriate vertex indices.

8.4.BFS

Here's an example of Breadth-First Search (BFS) implemented in Java using a class for a graph represented by an adjacency list:

```
import java.util.LinkedList;
import java.util.Queue;
class Graph {
    private int vertices;
    private LinkedList<Integer>[] adjacencyList;
    public Graph(int vertices) {
        this.vertices = vertices;
        this.adjacencyList = new LinkedList[vertices];
        for (int i = 0; i < vertices; i++) {
            adjacencyList[i] = new LinkedList<>();
        }
    }
    // Add an edge to the graph
    public void addEdge(int source, int destination) {
        if (source >= 0 && source < vertices && destination >= 0 && destination < vertices) {
            adjacencyList[source].add(destination);
        } else {
            System.out.println("Invalid vertices");
        }
    }
    // Perform BFS traversal starting from a given vertex
    public void BFS(int startVertex) {
        boolean[] visited = new boolean[vertices];
        // Create a queue for BFS
        Queue<Integer> queue = new LinkedList<>();
        // Mark the current node as visited and enqueue it
        visited[startVertex] = true;
        queue.add(startVertex);
        while (!queue.isEmpty()) {
            // Dequeue a vertex from the queue and print it
```

```
            int currentVertex = queue.poll();
            System.out.print(currentVertex + " ");
            // Get all adjacent vertices of the dequeued vertex
            // If an adjacent vertex is not visited, mark it as visited and enqueue it
            for (int neighbor : adjacencyList[currentVertex]) {
                if (!visited[neighbor]) {
                    visited[neighbor] = true;
                    queue.add(neighbor);
                }
            }
        }
    }
}
public class BFSExample {
    public static void main(String[] args) {
        // Example usage
        int numberOfVertices = 7;
        Graph graph = new Graph(numberOfVertices);
        // Add edges to the graph
        graph.addEdge(0, 1);
        graph.addEdge(0, 2);
        graph.addEdge(1, 3);
        graph.addEdge(1, 4);
        graph.addEdge(2, 5);
        graph.addEdge(2, 6);
        // Perform BFS starting from vertex 0
        System.out.println("BFS traversal starting from vertex 0:");
        graph.BFS(0);
    }}
```

In this example:

- The Graph class represents an undirected graph using an adjacency list.
- The BFS method performs Breadth-First Search starting from a given vertex. It uses a queue to keep track of vertices to visit.

- The addEdge method adds an edge between two vertices by adding the destination vertex to the source vertex's adjacency list.
- The main method demonstrates example usage by creating a graph, adding edges, and performing BFS starting from vertex 0.

You can customize the number of vertices and edges in the graph by modifying the numberOfVertices variable and calling the addEdge method with appropriate vertex indices.

8.5. Detect a cycle in a directed graph

Detecting a cycle in a directed graph can be done using Depth-First Search (DFS). If during the DFS traversal, you encounter a vertex that is already in the recursion stack, then there is a cycle. Below is an example of how you can implement cycle detection in a directed graph using a class in Java:

```
import java.util.*;
class Graph {
    private int vertices;
    private List<Integer>[] adjacencyList;
    public Graph(int vertices) {
        this.vertices = vertices;
        this.adjacencyList = new ArrayList[vertices];
        for (int i = 0; i < vertices; i++) {
            adjacencyList[i] = new ArrayList<>();
        }
    }
    // Add an edge to the graph
    public void addEdge(int source, int destination) {
        if (source >= 0 && source < vertices && destination >= 0 && destination < vertices) {
            adjacencyList[source].add(destination);
        } else {
            System.out.println("Invalid vertices");
        }
    }
    // Helper method for cycle detection using DFS
    private boolean isCyclicUtil(int currentVertex, boolean[] visited, boolean[] recStack) {
        visited[currentVertex] = true;
        recStack[currentVertex] = true;
        for (int neighbor : adjacencyList[currentVertex]) {
            if (!visited[neighbor]) {
                if (isCyclicUtil(neighbor, visited, recStack)) {
                    return true;
                }
```

```
        } else if (recStack[neighbor]) {
            return true;
        }
    }
    recStack[currentVertex] = false;
    return false;
}
// Check if the graph contains a cycle
public boolean isCyclic() {
    boolean[] visited = new boolean[vertices];
    boolean[] recStack = new boolean[vertices];
    for (int i = 0; i < vertices; i++) {
        if (!visited[i] && isCyclicUtil(i, visited, recStack)) {
            return true;
        }
    }
    return false;
}
}
public class CycleDetectionExample {
    public static void main(String[] args) {
        // Example usage
        int numberOfVertices = 4;
        Graph graph = new Graph(numberOfVertices);
        // Add edges to the graph
        graph.addEdge(0, 1);
        graph.addEdge(0, 2);
        graph.addEdge(1, 2);
        graph.addEdge(2, 0);
        graph.addEdge(2, 3);
        graph.addEdge(3, 3);
        // Check if the graph contains a cycle
        boolean hasCycle = graph.isCyclic();
```

```
        if (hasCycle) {
            System.out.println("The graph contains a cycle.");
        } else {
            System.out.println("The graph does not contain a cycle.");
        }
    }
}
```

In this example:

- The Graph class represents a directed graph using an adjacency list.
- The isCyclicUtil method is a recursive helper method that performs DFS and checks for cycles.
- The isCyclic method initializes arrays for visited nodes and the recursion stack and iterates through all vertices to check for cycles.
- The main method demonstrates example usage by creating a graph, adding edges, and checking if the graph contains a cycle.

You can customize the number of vertices and edges in the graph by modifying the numberOfVertices variable and calling the addEdge method with appropriate vertex indices.

8.6. Detect a cycle in a undirected graph

Detecting a cycle in an undirected graph can be done using Depth-First Search (DFS). If during the DFS traversal, you encounter a neighbor that is already visited but not the parent of the current node, then there is a cycle. Below is an example of how you can implement cycle detection in an undirected graph using a class in Java:

```
import java.util.ArrayList;
import java.util.List;
class Graph {
    private int vertices;
    private List<Integer>[] adjacencyList;
    public Graph(int vertices) {
        this.vertices = vertices;
        this.adjacencyList = new ArrayList[vertices];
        for (int i = 0; i < vertices; i++) {
            adjacencyList[i] = new ArrayList<>();
        }
    }
    // Add an edge to the graph
    public void addEdge(int source, int destination) {
        if (source >= 0 && source < vertices && destination >= 0 && destination < vertices) {
            adjacencyList[source].add(destination);
            adjacencyList[destination].add(source); // For undirected graph
        } else {
            System.out.println("Invalid vertices");
        }
    }
    // Helper method for cycle detection using DFS
    private boolean isCyclicUtil(int currentVertex, boolean[] visited, int parent) {
        visited[currentVertex] = true;
        for (int neighbor : adjacencyList[currentVertex]) {
            if (!visited[neighbor]) {
                if (isCyclicUtil(neighbor, visited, currentVertex)) {
                    return true;
```

```
                }
            } else if (neighbor != parent) {
                // If the neighbor is visited and not the parent of the current vertex, there is a cycle
                return true;
            }
        }
        return false;
    }
    // Check if the graph contains a cycle
    public boolean isCyclic() {
        boolean[] visited = new boolean[vertices];
        for (int i = 0; i < vertices; i++) {
            if (!visited[i] && isCyclicUtil(i, visited, -1)) {
                return true;
            }
        }
        return false;
    }
}
public class CycleDetectionUndirectedGraph {
    public static void main(String[] args) {
        // Example usage
        int numberOfVertices = 4;
        Graph graph = new Graph(numberOfVertices);
        // Add edges to the graph
        graph.addEdge(0, 1);
        graph.addEdge(1, 2);
        graph.addEdge(2, 0);
        graph.addEdge(1, 3);
        // Check if the graph contains a cycle
        boolean hasCycle = graph.isCyclic();
        if (hasCycle) {
            System.out.println("The graph contains a cycle.");
```

```
        } else {
            System.out.println("The graph does not contain a cycle.");
        }
    }
}
```

In this example:

- The Graph class represents an undirected graph using an adjacency list.
- The isCyclicUtil method is a recursive helper method that performs DFS and checks for cycles.
- The isCyclic method initializes an array for visited nodes and iterates through all vertices to check for cycles.
- The main method demonstrates example usage by creating a graph, adding edges, and checking if the graph contains a cycle.

You can customize the number of vertices and edges in the graph by modifying the numberOfVertices variable and calling the addEdge method with appropriate vertex indices.

8.7. Bellman –ford algorithm for finding the shortest path in a weighted graph

The Bellman-Ford algorithm is used to find the shortest paths from a source vertex to all other vertices in a weighted graph, even in the presence of negative weight edges (as long as there is no negative cycle). Below is an implementation of the Bellman-Ford algorithm in Java using a class for a weighted directed graph:

```
import java.util.Arrays;
class WeightedDirectedGraph {
    private int vertices;
    private int edges;
    private Edge[] edgeList;
    class Edge {
        int source, destination, weight;
        Edge() {
            source = destination = weight = 0;
        }
    }
    public WeightedDirectedGraph(int vertices, int edges) {
        this.vertices = vertices;
        this.edges = edges;
        this.edgeList = new Edge[edges];
        for (int i = 0; i < edges; ++i) {
            edgeList[i] = new Edge();
        }
    }
    // Add an edge to the graph
    public void addEdge(int index, int source, int destination, int weight) {
        if (index >= 0 && index < edges) {
            edgeList[index].source = source;
            edgeList[index].destination = destination;
            edgeList[index].weight = weight;
        } else {
            System.out.println("Invalid edge index");
        }
```

```
}
// Bellman-Ford algorithm to find the shortest paths
public void bellmanFord(int source) {
    int[] distance = new int[vertices];
    Arrays.fill(distance, Integer.MAX_VALUE);
    distance[source] = 0;
    // Relax all edges V-1 times
    for (int i = 1; i < vertices; ++i) {
        for (int j = 0; j < edges; ++j) {
            int u = edgeList[j].source;
            int v = edgeList[j].destination;
            int weight = edgeList[j].weight;
            if (distance[u] != Integer.MAX_VALUE && distance[u] + weight < distance[v]) {
                distance[v] = distance[u] + weight;
            }
        }
    }
    // Check for negative cycles
    for (int j = 0; j < edges; ++j) {
        int u = edgeList[j].source;
        int v = edgeList[j].destination;
        int weight = edgeList[j].weight;
        if (distance[u] != Integer.MAX_VALUE && distance[u] + weight < distance[v]) {
            System.out.println("Graph contains negative weight cycle");
            return;
        }
    }
    // Print the shortest distances
    printShortestDistances(distance, source);
}
// Print the shortest distances
private void printShortestDistances(int[] distance, int source) {
    System.out.println("Shortest distances from source " + source + ":");
```

```
        for (int i = 0; i < vertices; ++i) {
            System.out.println("To vertex " + i + ": " + distance[i]);
        }
    }
}
public class BellmanFordExample {
    public static void main(String[] args) {
        // Example usage
        int numberOfVertices = 5;
        int numberOfEdges = 8;
        WeightedDirectedGraph graph = new WeightedDirectedGraph(numberOfVertices,
numberOfEdges);
        // Add edges to the graph (index, source, destination, weight)
        graph.addEdge(0, 0, 1, -1);
        graph.addEdge(1, 0, 2, 4);
        graph.addEdge(2, 1, 2, 3);
        graph.addEdge(3, 1, 3, 2);
        graph.addEdge(4, 1, 4, 2);
        graph.addEdge(5, 3, 2, 5);
        graph.addEdge(6, 3, 1, 1);
        graph.addEdge(7, 4, 3, -3);
        // Perform Bellman-Ford algorithm from source vertex 0
        graph.bellmanFord(0);
    }
}
```

In this example:

- The WeightedDirectedGraph class represents a weighted directed graph using an edge list.
- The Edge class represents an edge with source, destination, and weight.
- The addEdge method adds an edge to the graph.
- The bellmanFord method performs the Bellman-Ford algorithm to find the shortest paths from the source vertex to all other vertices.

- The printShortestDistances method prints the shortest distances from the source vertex.
- The main method demonstrates example usage by creating a graph, adding edges, and performing the Bellman-Ford algorithm from source vertex 0.

8.8 Dijkstra's Algorithm

Dijkstra's algorithm is a popular algorithm for finding the shortest paths between nodes in a weighted graph. Below is an implementation of Dijkstra's algorithm in Java using a class for a weighted graph:

```
import java.util.*;
class WeightedGraph {
    private int vertices;
    private List<Edge>[] adjacencyList;
    class Edge {
        int destination, weight;
        Edge(int destination, int weight) {
            this.destination = destination;
            this.weight = weight;
        }
    }
    public WeightedGraph(int vertices) {
        this.vertices = vertices;
        this.adjacencyList = new ArrayList[vertices];

        for (int i = 0; i < vertices; i++) {
            adjacencyList[i] = new ArrayList<>();
        }
    }
    // Add an edge to the graph
    public void addEdge(int source, int destination, int weight) {
        adjacencyList[source].add(new Edge(destination, weight));
        adjacencyList[destination].add(new Edge(source, weight)); // For undirected graph
    }
    // Dijkstra's algorithm to find the shortest paths
    public void dijkstra(int source) {
        PriorityQueue<Node> minHeap = new
PriorityQueue<>(Comparator.comparingInt(node -> node.distance));
        int[] distance = new int[vertices];
```

```
    Arrays.fill(distance, Integer.MAX_VALUE);
    distance[source] = 0;
    minHeap.add(new Node(source, 0));
    while (!minHeap.isEmpty()) {
      Node currentNode = minHeap.poll();
      int u = currentNode.vertex;
      for (Edge neighbor : adjacencyList[u]) {
        int v = neighbor.destination;
        int weight = neighbor.weight;
        if (distance[u] != Integer.MAX_VALUE && distance[u] + weight < distance[v]) {
          distance[v] = distance[u] + weight;
          minHeap.add(new Node(v, distance[v]));
        }
      }
    }
    printShortestDistances(distance, source);
  }
  // Helper class for nodes in the priority queue
  class Node {
    int vertex, distance;
    Node(int vertex, int distance) {
      this.vertex = vertex;
      this.distance = distance;
    }
  }
  // Print the shortest distances
  private void printShortestDistances(int[] distance, int source) {
    System.out.println("Shortest distances from source " + source + ":");
    for (int i = 0; i < vertices; ++i) {
      System.out.println("To vertex " + i + ": " + distance[i]);
    }
  }
}
```

```
public class DijkstraExample {
    public static void main(String[] args) {
        // Example usage
        int numberOfVertices = 5;
        WeightedGraph graph = new WeightedGraph(numberOfVertices);
        // Add edges to the graph (source, destination, weight)
        graph.addEdge(0, 1, 2);
        graph.addEdge(0, 2, 4);
        graph.addEdge(1, 2, 1);
        graph.addEdge(1, 3, 7);
        graph.addEdge(2, 4, 3);
        graph.addEdge(3, 4, 1);
        // Perform Dijkstra's algorithm from source vertex 0
        graph.dijkstra(0);
    }
}
```

In this example:

- The WeightedGraph class represents a weighted graph using an adjacency list.
- The Edge class represents an edge with destination and weight.
- The addEdge method adds an edge to the graph.
- The dijkstra method performs Dijkstra's algorithm to find the shortest paths from the source vertex to all other vertices.
- The Node class is a helper class for nodes in the priority queue.
- The printShortestDistances method prints the shortest distances from the source vertex.
- The main method demonstrates example usage by creating a graph, adding edges, and performing Dijkstra's algorithm from source vertex 0.

8.9. Prim's Algorithm

Prim's algorithm is a popular algorithm for finding the minimum spanning tree (MST) of a connected, undirected graph with weighted edges. Below is an implementation of Prim's algorithm in Java using a class for a weighted graph:

```
import java.util.*;
class WeightedGraph {
    private int vertices;
    private List<Edge>[] adjacencyList;
    class Edge {
        int destination, weight;
        Edge(int destination, int weight) {
            this.destination = destination;
            this.weight = weight;
        }
    }
    public WeightedGraph(int vertices) {
        this.vertices = vertices;
        this.adjacencyList = new ArrayList[vertices];
        for (int i = 0; i < vertices; i++) {
            adjacencyList[i] = new ArrayList<>();
        }
    }
    // Add an edge to the graph
    public void addEdge(int source, int destination, int weight) {
        adjacencyList[source].add(new Edge(destination, weight));
        adjacencyList[destination].add(new Edge(source, weight)); // For undirected graph
    }
    // Prim's algorithm to find the minimum spanning tree
    public void prim() {
        PriorityQueue<Node> minHeap = new
PriorityQueue<>(Comparator.comparingInt(node -> node.key));
        boolean[] inMST = new boolean[vertices];
        int[] key = new int[vertices];
```

```
        int[] parent = new int[vertices];
        Arrays.fill(key, Integer.MAX_VALUE);
        Arrays.fill(parent, -1);
        key[0] = 0;
        minHeap.add(new Node(0, 0));
        while (!minHeap.isEmpty()) {
            Node currentNode = minHeap.poll();
            int u = currentNode.vertex;
            inMST[u] = true;
            for (Edge neighbor : adjacencyList[u]) {
                int v = neighbor.destination;
                int weight = neighbor.weight;
                if (!inMST[v] && weight < key[v]) {
                    key[v] = weight;
                    parent[v] = u;
                    minHeap.add(new Node(v, key[v]));
                }
            }
        }
        printMinimumSpanningTree(parent, key);
    }
    // Helper class for nodes in the priority queue
    class Node {
        int vertex, key;
        Node(int vertex, int key) {
            this.vertex = vertex;
            this.key = key;
        }
    }
    // Print the minimum spanning tree
    private void printMinimumSpanningTree(int[] parent, int[] key) {
        System.out.println("Edges in the minimum spanning tree:");
        for (int i = 1; i < vertices; ++i) {
```

```
            System.out.println("Edge: " + parent[i] + " - " + i + " Weight: " + key[i]);
        }
    }
}
public class PrimsAlgorithmExample {
    public static void main(String[] args) {
        // Example usage
        int numberOfVertices = 5;
        WeightedGraph graph = new WeightedGraph(numberOfVertices);
        // Add edges to the graph (source, destination, weight)
        graph.addEdge(0, 1, 2);
        graph.addEdge(0, 2, 3);
        graph.addEdge(1, 2, 1);
        graph.addEdge(1, 3, 3);
        graph.addEdge(2, 3, 4);
        graph.addEdge(3, 4, 2);
        // Perform Prim's algorithm to find the minimum spanning tree
        graph.prim();
    }
}
```

In this example:

- The WeightedGraph class represents a weighted graph using an adjacency list.
- The Edge class represents an edge with destination and weight.
- The addEdge method adds an edge to the graph.
- The prim method performs Prim's algorithm to find the minimum spanning tree.
- The Node class is a helper class for nodes in the priority queue.
- The printMinimumSpanningTree method prints the edges in the minimum spanning tree.
- The main method demonstrates example usage by creating a graph, adding edges, and performing Prim's algorithm.

8.10.Kruskal's algorithm for finding the minimum spanning tree

Kruskal's algorithm is a popular algorithm for finding the minimum spanning tree (MST) of a connected, undirected graph with weighted edges. Below is an implementation of Kruskal's algorithm in Java using a class for a weighted graph:

```
import java.util.*;
class WeightedGraph {
  private int vertices;
  private List<Edge> edgeList;
  class Edge implements Comparable<Edge> {
    int source, destination, weight;
    Edge(int source, int destination, int weight) {
      this.source = source;
      this.destination = destination;
      this.weight = weight;
    }
    @Override
    public int compareTo(Edge other) {
      return Integer.compare(this.weight, other.weight);
    }
  }
  public WeightedGraph(int vertices, int edges) {
    this.vertices = vertices;
    this.edgeList = new ArrayList<>(edges);
  }
  // Add an edge to the graph
  public void addEdge(int source, int destination, int weight) {
    edgeList.add(new Edge(source, destination, weight));
  }
  // Kruskal's algorithm to find the minimum spanning tree
  public void kruskal() {
    Collections.sort(edgeList);

    int[] parent = new int[vertices];
```

```
        for (int i = 0; i < vertices; ++i) {
            parent[i] = i;
        }
        List<Edge> minimumSpanningTree = new ArrayList<>();
        for (Edge edge : edgeList) {
            int root1 = find(parent, edge.source);
            int root2 = find(parent, edge.destination);
            if (root1 != root2) {
                minimumSpanningTree.add(edge);
                union(parent, root1, root2);
            }
        }
        printMinimumSpanningTree(minimumSpanningTree);
    }
    // Find the root of the set containing a particular element
    private int find(int[] parent, int vertex) {
        if (parent[vertex] != vertex) {
            parent[vertex] = find(parent, parent[vertex]);
        }
        return parent[vertex];
    }
    // Union of two sets
    private void union(int[] parent, int root1, int root2) {
        parent[root1] = root2;
    }
    // Print the minimum spanning tree
    private void printMinimumSpanningTree(List<Edge> minimumSpanningTree) {
        System.out.println("Edges in the minimum spanning tree:");
        for (Edge edge : minimumSpanningTree) {
            System.out.println("Edge: " + edge.source + " - " + edge.destination + " Weight: " +
edge.weight);
        }
    }
```

```
}
public class KruskalsAlgorithmExample {
    public static void main(String[] args) {
        // Example usage
        int numberOfVertices = 5;
        int numberOfEdges = 7;
        WeightedGraph graph = new WeightedGraph(numberOfVertices, numberOfEdges);
        // Add edges to the graph (source, destination, weight)
        graph.addEdge(0, 1, 2);
        graph.addEdge(0, 2, 4);
        graph.addEdge(1, 2, 1);
        graph.addEdge(1, 3, 7);
        graph.addEdge(2, 3, 4);
        graph.addEdge(2, 4, 3);
        graph.addEdge(3, 4, 1);
        // Perform Kruskal's algorithm to find the minimum spanning tree
        graph.kruskal();
    }
}
```

In this example:

- The WeightedGraph class represents a weighted graph using an edge list.
- The Edge class represents an edge with source, destination, and weight. It implements Comparable to enable sorting based on weight.
- The addEdge method adds an edge to the graph.
- The kruskal method performs Kruskal's algorithm to find the minimum spanning tree.
- The find method finds the root of the set containing a particular element.
- The union method performs the union of two sets.
- The printMinimumSpanningTree method prints the edges in the minimum spanning tree.
- The main method demonstrates example usage by creating a graph, adding edges, and performing Kruskal's algorithm.

9.HASHING

9.1. Implement a hash table

Below is a simple implementation of a hash table in Java using a class. In this example, I'm using separate chaining for handling collisions. The hash table has methods for insertion, retrieval, and deletion of key-value pairs.

```
import java.util.LinkedList;
class HashTable<K, V> {
    private static final int DEFAULT_CAPACITY = 10;
    private LinkedList<Entry<K, V>>[] table;
    private int size;
    static class Entry<K, V> {
        K key;
        V value;
        Entry(K key, V value) {
            this.key = key;
            this.value = value;
        }
    }
    public HashTable() {
        this(DEFAULT_CAPACITY);
    }
    public HashTable(int capacity) {
        table = new LinkedList[capacity];
        size = 0;
    }
    private int hash(K key) {
        return key.hashCode() % table.length;
    }
    public void put(K key, V value) {
        int index = hash(key);
        if (table[index] == null) {
            table[index] = new LinkedList<>();
        }
```

```
        // Check if the key already exists, and if so, update the value
        for (Entry<K, V> entry : table[index]) {
            if (entry.key.equals(key)) {
                entry.value = value;
                return;
            }
        }
        // Key not found, add a new entry
        table[index].add(new Entry<>(key, value));
        size++;
        // Optional: Resize the table if it exceeds a certain load factor
        if ((double) size / table.length > 0.75) {
            resize();
        }
    }
    public V get(K key) {
        int index = hash(key);
        LinkedList<Entry<K, V>> list = table[index];
        if (list != null) {
            for (Entry<K, V> entry : list) {
                if (entry.key.equals(key)) {
                    return entry.value;
                }
            }
        }
        return null; // Key not found
    }
    public void remove(K key) {
        int index = hash(key);
        LinkedList<Entry<K, V>> list = table[index];
        if (list != null) {
            for (Entry<K, V> entry : list) {
                if (entry.key.equals(key)) {
```

```
                list.remove(entry);
                size--;
                return;
            }
        }
    }
}
private void resize() {
    LinkedList<Entry<K, V>>[] newTable = new LinkedList[table.length * 2];
    for (LinkedList<Entry<K, V>> list : table) {
        if (list != null) {
            for (Entry<K, V> entry : list) {
                int newIndex = entry.key.hashCode() % newTable.length;
                if (newTable[newIndex] == null) {
                    newTable[newIndex] = new LinkedList<>();
                }
                newTable[newIndex].add(entry);
            }
        }
    }
    table = newTable;
}
public void printTable() {
    for (int i = 0; i < table.length; i++) {
        System.out.print("Bucket " + i + ": ");
        LinkedList<Entry<K, V>> list = table[i];
        if (list != null) {
            for (Entry<K, V> entry : list) {
                System.out.print("(" + entry.key + ", " + entry.value + ") ");
            }
        }
        System.out.println();
    }
```

```
    }
}
public class HashTableExample {
    public static void main(String[] args) {
        HashTable<String, Integer> hashTable = new HashTable<>();
        hashTable.put("one", 1);
        hashTable.put("two", 2);
        hashTable.put("three", 3);
        hashTable.put("four", 4);
        hashTable.put("five", 5);
        System.out.println("Original Hash Table:");
        hashTable.printTable();
        System.out.println("\nValue for key 'three': " + hashTable.get("three"));
        hashTable.remove("two");
        System.out.println("\nHash Table after removing key 'two':");
        hashTable.printTable();
    }
}
```

This example includes a basic HashTable class with methods for put, get, and remove. The Entry class is an inner class representing key-value pairs. The resize method is used to double the size of the hash table when the load factor exceeds 0.75. The printTable method is included for visualizing the contents of the hash table.

9.2. Resolve collisions using open addressing

Open addressing is a technique for resolving collisions in hash tables by probing into alternative positions when a collision occurs. Here's an example implementation of a hash table using open addressing (linear probing) in Java:

```
class OpenAddressingHashTable<K, V> {
    private static final int DEFAULT_CAPACITY = 10;
    private Entry<K, V>[] table;
    private int size;
    static class Entry<K, V> {
        K key;
        V value;
        Entry(K key, V value) {
            this.key = key;
            this.value = value;
        }
    }
    public OpenAddressingHashTable() {
        this(DEFAULT_CAPACITY);
    }
    public OpenAddressingHashTable(int capacity) {
        table = new Entry[capacity];
        size = 0;
    }
    private int hash(K key) {
        return key.hashCode() % table.length;
    }
    private int probe(int hash, int i) {
        return (hash + i) % table.length; // Linear probing
        // Other probing techniques (e.g., quadratic probing, double hashing) can also be used
    }
    public void put(K key, V value) {
        int hash = hash(key);
        int i = 0;
```

```
        while (table[hash] != null) {
            if (table[hash].key.equals(key)) {
                table[hash].value = value; // Update value if the key already exists
                return;
            }
            i++;
            hash = probe(hash, i);
        }
        table[hash] = new Entry<>(key, value);
        size++;
        // Optional: Resize the table if it exceeds a certain load factor
        if ((double) size / table.length > 0.75) {
            resize();
        }
    }
    public V get(K key) {
        int hash = hash(key);
        int i = 0;
        while (table[hash] != null) {
            if (table[hash].key.equals(key)) {
                return table[hash].value;
            }
            i++;
            hash = probe(hash, i);
        }
        return null; // Key not found
    }
    public void remove(K key) {
        int hash = hash(key);
        int i = 0;
        while (table[hash] != null) {
            if (table[hash].key.equals(key)) {
                table[hash] = null; // Mark the entry as deleted
```

```
                size--;
                return;
            }
            i++;
            hash = probe(hash, i);
        }
    }
    private void resize() {
        Entry<K, V>[] newTable = new Entry[table.length * 2];
        for (Entry<K, V> entry : table) {
            if (entry != null) {
                int hash = hash(entry.key);
                int i = 0;
                while (newTable[hash] != null) {
                    i++;
                    hash = probe(hash, i);
                }
                newTable[hash] = entry;
            }
        }
        table = newTable;
    }
    public void printTable() {
        System.out.println("Hash Table:");
        for (int i = 0; i < table.length; i++) {
            if (table[i] != null) {
                System.out.println("Index " + i + ": (" + table[i].key + ", " + table[i].value + ")");
            } else {
                System.out.println("Index " + i + ": null");
            }
        }
    }
}
```

```
public class OpenAddressingHashTableExample {
    public static void main(String[] args) {
        OpenAddressingHashTable<String, Integer> hashTable = new
OpenAddressingHashTable<>();
        hashTable.put("one", 1);
        hashTable.put("two", 2);
        hashTable.put("three", 3);
        hashTable.put("four", 4);
        hashTable.put("five", 5);
        System.out.println("Original Hash Table:");
        hashTable.printTable();
        System.out.println("\nValue for key 'three': " + hashTable.get("three"));
        hashTable.remove("two");
        System.out.println("\nHash Table after removing key 'two':");
        hashTable.printTable();
    }
}
```

This example includes an OpenAddressingHashTable class with methods for put, get, and remove. The Entry class is an inner class representing key-value pairs. The probe method is used for linear probing, but you can modify it for other probing techniques. The resize method is included for doubling the size of the hash table when thc load factor exceeds 0.75. The printTable method is included for visualizing the contents of the hash table.

9.3. Implement basic hash functions

Hash functions are crucial for hash tables. Below is an example implementation of a simple hash function using a class in Java. This example uses the division method for simplicity:

```
class BasicHashFunction {
    private static final int DEFAULT_CAPACITY = 10;
    private int capacity;
    public BasicHashFunction() {
        this(DEFAULT_CAPACITY);
    }
    public BasicHashFunction(int capacity) {
        this.capacity = capacity;
    }
    // Division method hash function
    public int hash(int key) {
        return key % capacity;
    }
    public void setCapacity(int newCapacity) {
        this.capacity = newCapacity;
    }
}
public class BasicHashFunctionExample {
    public static void main(String[] args) {
        BasicHashFunction hashFunction = new BasicHashFunction();
        int key1 = 42;
        int key2 = 19;
        System.out.println("Hash value for key " + key1 + ": " + hashFunction.hash(key1));
        System.out.println("Hash value for key " + key2 + ": " + hashFunction.hash(key2));
        // Adjusting the capacity
        hashFunction.setCapacity(20);
        System.out.println("\nHash value for key " + key1 + ": " + hashFunction.hash(key1));
        System.out.println("Hash value for key " + key2 + ": " + hashFunction.hash(key2));
    }
```

```
}
```

In this example:

- The BasicHashFunction class has a simple hash function using the division method (key % capacity).
- The hash method calculates the hash value for a given key.
- The setCapacity method allows changing the capacity of the hash function.

You can replace the division method with other hash functions based on your specific requirements. Keep in mind that more advanced hash functions (e.g., cryptographic hash functions) may be needed for security or certain applications.

9.4. Perform insert, delete and search operations in a hash table

Below is an example implementation of a hash table in Java with methods for insert, delete, and search operations:

```
import java.util.LinkedList;
class HashTable<K, V> {
    private static final int DEFAULT_CAPACITY = 10;
    private LinkedList<Entry<K, V>>[] table;
    private int size;
    static class Entry<K, V> {
        K key;
        V value;
        Entry(K key, V value) {
            this.key = key;
            this.value = value;
        }
    }
    public HashTable() {
        this(DEFAULT_CAPACITY);
    }
    public HashTable(int capacity) {
        table = new LinkedList[capacity];
        size = 0;
    }
    private int hash(K key) {
        return key.hashCode() % table.length;
    }
    public void put(K key, V value) {
        int index = hash(key);
        if (table[index] == null) {
            table[index] = new LinkedList<>();
        }
        // Check if the key already exists, and if so, update the value
        for (Entry<K, V> entry : table[index]) {
```

```
            if (entry.key.equals(key)) {
                entry.value = value;
                return;
            }
        }
        // Key not found, add a new entry
        table[index].add(new Entry<>(key, value));
        size++;
        // Optional: Resize the table if it exceeds a certain load factor
        if ((double) size / table.length > 0.75) {
            resize();
        }
    }
    public V get(K key) {
        int index = hash(key);
        LinkedList<Entry<K, V>> list = table[index];
        if (list != null) {
            for (Entry<K, V> entry : list) {
                if (entry.key.equals(key)) {
                    return entry.value;
                }
            }
        }
        return null; // Key not found
    }
    public void remove(K key) {
        int index = hash(key);
        LinkedList<Entry<K, V>> list = table[index];
        if (list != null) {
            for (Entry<K, V> entry : list) {
                if (entry.key.equals(key)) {
                    list.remove(entry);
                    size--;
```

```
                return;
            }
        }
    }
}
private void resize() {
    LinkedList<Entry<K, V>>[] newTable = new LinkedList[table.length * 2];
    for (LinkedList<Entry<K, V>> list : table) {
        if (list != null) {
            for (Entry<K, V> entry : list) {
                int newIndex = entry.key.hashCode() % newTable.length;
                if (newTable[newIndex] == null) {
                    newTable[newIndex] = new LinkedList<>();
                }
                newTable[newIndex].add(entry);
            }
        }
    }
    table = newTable;
}
public void printTable() {
    System.out.println("Hash Table:");
    for (int i = 0; i < table.length; i++) {
        if (table[i] != null) {
            for (Entry<K, V> entry : table[i]) {
                System.out.println("Index " + i + ": (" + entry.key + ", " + entry.value + ")");
            }
        } else {
            System.out.println("Index " + i + ": null");
        }
    }
}
}
```

```
public class HashTableOperationsExample {
    public static void main(String[] args) {
        HashTable<String, Integer> hashTable = new HashTable<>();
        hashTable.put("one", 1);
        hashTable.put("two", 2);
        hashTable.put("three", 3);
        hashTable.put("four", 4);
        hashTable.put("five", 5);
        System.out.println("Original Hash Table:");
        hashTable.printTable();
        System.out.println("\nValue for key 'three': " + hashTable.get("three"));
        hashTable.remove("two");
        System.out.println("\nHash Table after removing key 'two':");
        hashTable.printTable();
    }
}
```

This example includes a HashTable class with methods for put, get, and remove. The Entry class is an inner class representing key-value pairs. The resize method is included for doubling the size of the hash table when the load factor exceeds 0.75. The printTable method is included for visualizing the contents of the hash table.

10.HEAP

10.1. Implement a binary heap (Min and Max heap)

Below is an implementation of both Min Heap and Max Heap using a class in Java:

```
import java.util.Arrays;
class BinaryHeap {
    private int[] heap;
    private int size;
    private int capacity;
    private boolean isMaxHeap;
    public BinaryHeap(int capacity, boolean isMaxHeap) {
        this.capacity = capacity;
        this.isMaxHeap = isMaxHeap;
        this.heap = new int[capacity];
        this.size = 0;
    }
    public BinaryHeap(boolean isMaxHeap) {
        this(10, isMaxHeap); // Default capacity is 10
    }
    public BinaryHeap(int capacity) {
        this(capacity, false); // Default is Min Heap
    }
    public BinaryHeap() {
        this(10, false); // Default is Min Heap with capacity 10
    }
    private int parent(int index) {
        return (index - 1) / 2;
    }
    private int leftChild(int index) {
        return 2 * index + 1;
    }
    private int rightChild(int index) {
        return 2 * index + 2;
    }
```

```
    private void swap(int i, int j) {
        int temp = heap[i];
        heap[i] = heap[j];
        heap[j] = temp;
    }
    private boolean shouldSwap(int parent, int child) {
        return (isMaxHeap && heap[parent] < heap[child]) || (!isMaxHeap && heap[parent] >
heap[child]);
    }
    public void insert(int value) {
        if (size == capacity) {
            resize();
        }
       heap[size] = value;
        size++;
        int currentIndex = size - 1;
        int parentIndex = parent(currentIndex);
        while (currentIndex > 0 && shouldSwap(parentIndex, currentIndex)) {
            swap(parentIndex, currentIndex);
            currentIndex = parentIndex;
            parentIndex = parent(currentIndex);
        }
    }
    public int peek() {
        if (size == 0) {
            throw new IllegalStateException("Heap is empty");
        }
        return heap[0];
    }
    public int extract() {
        if (size == 0) {
            throw new IllegalStateException("Heap is empty");
        }
```

```
        int root = heap[0];
        heap[0] = heap[size - 1];
        size--;
        heapifyDown(0);
        return root;
    }
    private void heapifyDown(int index) {
        int leftChildIndex = leftChild(index);
        int rightChildIndex = rightChild(index);
        int swapIndex = index;
        if (leftChildIndex < size && shouldSwap(index, leftChildIndex)) {
            swapIndex = leftChildIndex;
        }
        if (rightChildIndex < size && shouldSwap(swapIndex, rightChildIndex)) {
            swapIndex = rightChildIndex;
        }
        if (index != swapIndex) {
            swap(index, swapIndex);
            heapifyDown(swapIndex);
        }
    }
    private void resize() {
        capacity *= 2;
        heap = Arrays.copyOf(heap, capacity);
    }
    public int size() {
        return size;
    }
    public boolean isEmpty() {
        return size == 0;
    }
    public void printHeap() {
        System.out.print("Heap: ");
```

```
        for (int i = 0; i < size; i++) {
            System.out.print(heap[i] + " ");
        }
        System.out.println();
    }
}
public class HeapExample {
    public static void main(String[] args) {
        // Example of Min Heap
        BinaryHeap minHeap = new BinaryHeap();
        minHeap.insert(4);
        minHeap.insert(8);
        minHeap.insert(2);
        minHeap.insert(1);
        minHeap.insert(9);
        System.out.println("Min Heap:");
        minHeap.printHeap();
        while (!minHeap.isEmpty()) {
            System.out.println("Extracted: " + minHeap.extract());
        }
        // Example of Max Heap
        BinaryHeap maxHeap = new BinaryHeap(10, true);
        maxHeap.insert(4);
        maxHeap.insert(8);
        maxHeap.insert(2);
        maxHeap.insert(1);
        maxHeap.insert(9);
        System.out.println("\nMax Heap:");
        maxHeap.printHeap();
        while (!maxHeap.isEmpty()) {
            System.out.println("Extracted: " + maxHeap.extract());
        }
    }
```

```
}
```

This example includes a BinaryHeap class that can be used to create both Min Heap and Max Heap. The insert, peek, and extract methods are implemented, and the heapifyDown operation is used for maintaining the heap property. The resize method is used to dynamically resize the array when needed.

In the HeapExample class, you can see examples of both Min Heap and Max Heap. The insert method is used to insert elements, and the peek and extract methods are used to get the minimum or maximum value from the heap. The printHeap method is included for visualizing the contents of the heap.

10.2. Heap sort

Below is an implementation of the Heap Sort algorithm using a class in Java. In this example, the class named HeapSort contains methods for building a max heap, heap sorting, and printing the sorted array.

```
import java.util.Arrays;
class HeapSort {
   public static void sort(int[] array) {
      int n = array.length;
      // Build max heap
      for (int i = n / 2 - 1; i >= 0; i--) {
         heapify(array, n, i);
      }
      // Extract elements one by one from the heap
      for (int i = n - 1; i > 0; i--) {
         // Swap the root (maximum element) with the last element
         int temp = array[0];
         array[0] = array[i];
         array[i] = temp;

         // Call heapify on the reduced heap
         heapify(array, i, 0);
      }
   }
   private static void heapify(int[] array, int n, int root) {
      int largest = root;
      int leftChild = 2 * root + 1;
      int rightChild = 2 * root + 2;
      if (leftChild < n && array[leftChild] > array[largest]) {
         largest = leftChild;
      }
      if (rightChild < n && array[rightChild] > array[largest]) {
         largest = rightChild;
      }
```

```
        if (largest != root) {
            // Swap root with the largest element
            int temp = array[root];
            array[root] = array[largest];
            array[largest] = temp;
            // Recursively heapify the affected sub-tree
            heapify(array, n, largest);
        }
    }
    public static void printArray(int[] array) {
        System.out.println("Sorted Array: " + Arrays.toString(array));
    }
}
public class HeapSortExample {
    public static void main(String[] args) {
        int[] array = {12, 11, 13, 5, 6, 7};
                System.out.println("Original Array: " + Arrays.toString(array));
        // Perform Heap Sort
        HeapSort.sort(array);
        // Print the sorted array
        HeapSort.printArray(array);
    }
}
```

In this example:

- The HeapSort class contains a static method sort for performing Heap Sort, a private method heapify for maintaining the max heap property, and a printArray method for printing the sorted array.
- The HeapSortExample class demonstrates the usage of the HeapSort class by creating an array, performing Heap Sort, and printing the sorted array.
- When you run this program, it will output the original array, perform Heap Sort, and then print the sorted array.

11.PRIORITY QUEUE

11.1. Implement a priority queue using a heap data structure

Below is an implementation of a priority queue using a max heap data structure in Java. The PriorityQueue class includes methods for adding elements (enqueue), removing the highest priority element (dequeue), and checking if the queue is empty.

```
import java.util.Arrays;
class MaxHeapPriorityQueue {
    private int[] heap;
    private int size;
    private int capacity;
    public MaxHeapPriorityQueue(int capacity) {
        this.capacity = capacity;
        this.heap = new int[capacity];
        this.size = 0;
    }
    private int parent(int index) {
        return (index - 1) / 2;
    }
    private int leftChild(int index) {
        return 2 * index + 1;
    }
    private int rightChild(int index) {
        return 2 * index + 2;
    }
    private void swap(int i, int j) {
        int temp = heap[i];
        heap[i] = heap[j];
        heap[j] = temp;
    }
    private void heapifyUp(int index) {
        int currentIndex = index;
        int parentIndex = parent(currentIndex);
        while (currentIndex > 0 && heap[currentIndex] > heap[parentIndex]) {
```

```
            swap(currentIndex, parentIndex);
            currentIndex = parentIndex;
            parentIndex = parent(currentIndex);
        }
    }
    private void heapifyDown(int index) {
        int leftChildIndex = leftChild(index);
        int rightChildIndex = rightChild(index);
        int swapIndex = index;
        if (leftChildIndex < size && heap[leftChildIndex] > heap[swapIndex]) {
            swapIndex = leftChildIndex;
        }
        if (rightChildIndex < size && heap[rightChildIndex] > heap[swapIndex]) {
            swapIndex = rightChildIndex;
        }
        if (index != swapIndex) {
            swap(index, swapIndex);
            heapifyDown(swapIndex);
        }
    }
    public void enqueue(int value) {
        if (size == capacity) {
            resize();
        }
        heap[size] = value;
        size++;
        heapifyUp(size - 1);
    }
    public int dequeue() {
        if (size == 0) {
            throw new IllegalStateException("Priority queue is empty");
        }
        int root = heap[0];
```

```
        heap[0] = heap[size - 1];
        size--;
        heapifyDown(0);
        return root;
    }
    private void resize() {
        capacity *= 2;
        heap = Arrays.copyOf(heap, capacity);
    }
    public boolean isEmpty() {
        return size == 0;
    }
    public void printQueue() {
        System.out.print("Priority Queue: ");
        for (int i = 0; i < size; i++) {
            System.out.print(heap[i] + " ");
        }
        System.out.println();
    }
}
public class PriorityQueueExample {
    public static void main(String[] args) {
        MaxHeapPriorityQueue priorityQueue = new MaxHeapPriorityQueue(10);
        priorityQueue.enqueue(4);
        priorityQueue.enqueue(8);
        priorityQueue.enqueue(2);
        priorityQueue.enqueue(1);
        priorityQueue.enqueue(9);

        System.out.println("Original Priority Queue:");
        priorityQueue.printQueue();

        while (!priorityQueue.isEmpty()) {
```

```
            System.out.println("Dequeued: " + priorityQueue.dequeue());
        }
    }
}
```

In this example:

- The MaxHeapPriorityQueue class has methods for enqueueing (adding elements), dequeuing (removing the highest priority element), and checking if the queue is empty.
- The enqueue method adds an element to the priority queue and maintains the max heap property by calling heapifyUp.
- The dequeue method removes the highest priority element (the maximum value) from the priority queue and maintains the max heap property by calling heapifyDown.
- The resize method is used to dynamically resize the array when needed.
- The PriorityQueueExample class demonstrates the usage of the MaxHeapPriorityQueue by enqueuing elements, printing the priority queue, and dequeuing elements.

11.2. Use a priority queue to solve a real world problem like task scheduling

Let's consider a simplified example of task scheduling using a priority queue in Java. In this example, tasks have associated priorities, and we want to execute tasks in order of their priorities.

```
import java.util.PriorityQueue;
class Task implements Comparable<Task> {
   private String name;
   private int priority;
   public Task(String name, int priority) {
      this.name = name;
      this.priority = priority;
   }
   public String getName() {
      return name;
   }
   public int getPriority() {
      return priority;
   }
   @Override
   public int compareTo(Task other) {
      // Higher priority tasks come first
      return Integer.compare(other.getPriority(), this.priority);
   }
   @Override
   public String toString() {
      return "Task: " + name + " (Priority: " + priority + ")";
   }
}
class TaskScheduler {
   private PriorityQueue<Task> priorityQueue;

   public TaskScheduler() {
      this.priorityQueue = new PriorityQueue<>();
```

```
    }
    public void scheduleTask(Task task) {
        priorityQueue.add(task);
    }
    public Task getNextTask() {
        if (priorityQueue.isEmpty()) {
            return null;
        }
        return priorityQueue.poll();
    }
    public boolean hasTasks() {
        return !priorityQueue.isEmpty();
    }
}
public class TaskSchedulingExample {
    public static void main(String[] args) {
        TaskScheduler taskScheduler = new TaskScheduler();
        // Schedule tasks with priorities
        taskScheduler.scheduleTask(new Task("Task A", 3));
        taskScheduler.scheduleTask(new Task("Task B", 1));
        taskScheduler.scheduleTask(new Task("Task C", 5));
        taskScheduler.scheduleTask(new Task("Task D", 2));
        // Execute tasks in order of priority
        while (taskScheduler.hasTasks()) {
            Task nextTask = taskScheduler.getNextTask();
            System.out.println("Executing: " + nextTask);
        }
    }
}
```

In this example:

- The Task class represents a task with a name and priority. It implements the Comparable interface to define the natural ordering based on priority.

- The TaskScheduler class uses a PriorityQueue to schedule and execute tasks in order of priority.
- The scheduleTask method adds a task to the priority queue.
- The getNextTask method retrieves and removes the highest priority task from the priority queue.
- The hasTasks method checks if there are tasks in the queue.
- In the main method, tasks are scheduled with different priorities, and then the tasks are executed in order of their priorities.

This is a simplified example, and in a real-world scenario, tasks and priorities might be more complex, and additional features could be added to the classes to handle more detailed scheduling requirements.

12.DYNAMIC PROGRAMMING

12.1. Fibonacci Series

Below is an example implementation of generating Fibonacci series using dynamic programming in Java with a class named FibonacciGenerator.

```
import java.util.Arrays;
class FibonacciGenerator {
    private long[] memo;
    public FibonacciGenerator(int n) {
        memo = new long[n + 1];
        Arrays.fill(memo, -1); // Initialize memoization array with -1
    }
    public long generateFibonacci(int n) {
        if (n < 0) {
            throw new IllegalArgumentException("Input should be a non-negative integer");
        }
        return fibonacci(n);
    }
    private long fibonacci(int n) {
        if (n <= 1) {
            return n;
        }
        // Check if the result is already memoized
        if (memo[n] != -1) {
            return memo[n];
        }
        // Calculate Fibonacci number and memoize the result
        memo[n] = fibonacci(n - 1) + fibonacci(n - 2);
        return memo[n];
    }
    public void printFibonacciSeries(int n) {
        System.out.print("Fibonacci Series up to " + n + ": ");
        for (int i = 0; i <= n; i++) {
            System.out.print(generateFibonacci(i) + " ");
```

```
        }
        System.out.println();
    }
}
public class FibonacciExample {
    public static void main(String[] args) {
        int n = 10; // Adjust the value of n as needed
        FibonacciGenerator fibonacciGenerator = new FibonacciGenerator(n);
        long result = fibonacciGenerator.generateFibonacci(n);
        System.out.println("Fibonacci(" + n + ") = " + result);
        fibonacciGenerator.printFibonacciSeries(n);
    }
}
```

In this example:

- The FibonacciGenerator class contains a memo array for memoization.
- The generateFibonacci method initializes the memoization array and calls the fibonacci method to generate the Fibonacci number for a given n.
- The fibonacci method implements the dynamic programming approach with memoization to avoid redundant calculations.
- The printFibonacciSeries method prints the Fibonacci series up to the specified value of n.
- Feel free to adjust the value of n in the main method to generate the Fibonacci series up to a different index. This implementation improves the efficiency of calculating Fibonacci numbers by avoiding redundant computations using memoization.

12.2. Longest common subsequence problem

Below is an example implementation of the Longest Common Subsequence (LCS) problem using dynamic programming in Java with a class named LCSFinder.

```
class LCSFinder {
    public static String findLCS(String str1, String str2) {
        int m = str1.length();
        int n = str2.length();
        int[][] dp = new int[m + 1][n + 1];
        // Build the LCS matrix using dynamic programming
        for (int i = 1; i <= m; i++) {
            for (int j = 1; j <= n; j++) {
                if (str1.charAt(i - 1) == str2.charAt(j - 1)) {
                    dp[i][j] = dp[i - 1][j - 1] + 1;
                } else {
                    dp[i][j] = Math.max(dp[i - 1][j], dp[i][j - 1]);
                }
            }
        }
        // Reconstruct the LCS from the matrix
        int i = m;
        int j = n;
        StringBuilder lcs = new StringBuilder();
        while (i > 0 && j > 0) {
            if (str1.charAt(i - 1) == str2.charAt(j - 1)) {
                lcs.insert(0, str1.charAt(i - 1));
                i--;
                j--;
            } else if (dp[i - 1][j] > dp[i][j - 1]) {
                i--;
            } else {
                j--;
            }
        }
```

```
        return lcs.toString();
    }
}
public class LCSExample {
    public static void main(String[] args) {
        String str1 = "ABCD";
        String str2 = "ACDF";
        LCSFinder lcsFinder = new LCSFinder();
        String lcs = lcsFinder.findLCS(str1, str2);
        System.out.println("Longest Common Subsequence: " + lcs);
    }
}
```

In this example:

- The LCSFinder class contains a static method findLCS that takes two strings (str1 and str2) as input and returns the Longest Common Subsequence (LCS) between them.
- The dynamic programming approach is used to build a matrix (dp) to store the length of the LCS for each pair of substrings.
- The matrix is filled iteratively, and then the LCS is reconstructed by backtracking through the matrix.
- The main method in the LCSExample class demonstrates the usage of the LCSFinder to find the LCS of two example strings ("ABCD" and "ACDF").

12.3. Knapsack problem

The Knapsack problem is a classic optimization problem where the goal is to maximize the total value of items selected, subject to a constraint on the total weight. Below is an example implementation of the 0/1 Knapsack problem using dynamic programming in Java with a class named KnapsackSolver.

```
class KnapsackSolver {
    public static int knapsack(int[] weights, int[] values, int capacity) {
        int n = weights.length;
        int[][] dp = new int[n + 1][capacity + 1];
        // Build the DP table using dynamic programming
        for (int i = 1; i <= n; i++) {
            for (int w = 1; w <= capacity; w++) {
                if (weights[i - 1] <= w) {
                    dp[i][w] = Math.max(values[i - 1] + dp[i - 1][w - weights[i - 1]], dp[i - 1][w]);
                } else {
                    dp[i][w] = dp[i - 1][w];
                }
            }
        }
        return dp[n][capacity];
    }
}
public class KnapsackExample {
    public static void main(String[] args) {
        int[] weights = {2, 3, 4, 5};
        int[] values = {3, 4, 5, 6};
        int capacity = 5;
        KnapsackSolver knapsackSolver = new KnapsackSolver();
        int maxValue = knapsackSolver.knapsack(weights, values, capacity);
        System.out.println("Maximum value that can be obtained: " + maxValue);
    }}
```

In this example:

- The KnapsackSolver class contains a static method knapsack that takes arrays of weights, values, and the capacity of the knapsack as input and returns the maximum value that can be obtained.
- The dynamic programming approach is used to build a table (dp) to store the maximum value for each subproblem.
- The table is filled iteratively, and the final result is obtained from the bottom-right cell of the table.
- The main method in the KnapsackExample class demonstrates the usage of the KnapsackSolver to find the maximum value for a given set of weights, values, and capacity.

Feel free to modify the weights, values, and capacity in the main method to solve the Knapsack problem for different scenarios.

13. TRIE IMPLEMENTATION

13.1. Implement a trie data structure for efficient string storage and retrieval

Below is an implementation of a Trie data structure in Java using a class named TrieNode. The Trie class includes methods for inserting, searching, and deleting strings in the Trie.

```
class TrieNode {
    private TrieNode[] children;
    private boolean isEndOfWord;
    public TrieNode() {
        this.children = new TrieNode[26]; // Assuming lowercase English letters
        this.isEndOfWord = false;
    }
    public TrieNode getChild(char ch) {
        return children[ch - 'a'];
    }
    public void setChild(char ch, TrieNode node) {
        children[ch - 'a'] = node;
    }
    public boolean isEndOfWord() {
        return isEndOfWord;
    }
    public void setEndOfWord(boolean endOfWord) {
        isEndOfWord = endOfWord;
    }
}
public class Trie {
    private TrieNode root;
    public Trie() {
        this.root = new TrieNode();
    }
    public void insert(String word) {
        TrieNode node = root;
        for (char ch : word.toCharArray()) {
```

```
            if (node.getChild(ch) == null) {
                node.setChild(ch, new TrieNode());
            }
            node = node.getChild(ch);
        }
        node.setEndOfWord(true);
    }
    public boolean search(String word) {
        TrieNode node = searchNode(word);
        return node != null && node.isEndOfWord();
    }
    public boolean startsWith(String prefix) {
        return searchNode(prefix) != null;
    }
    private TrieNode searchNode(String word) {
        TrieNode node = root;
        for (char ch : word.toCharArray()) {
            node = node.getChild(ch);
            if (node == null) {
                return null; // Prefix not found
            }
        }
        return node;
    }
    public void delete(String word) {
        delete(root, word, 0);
    }
    private boolean delete(TrieNode node, String word, int depth) {
        if (node == null) {
            return false;
        }
        if (depth == word.length()) {
            if (!node.isEndOfWord()) {
```

```
                return false; // Word not found
            }
            node.setEndOfWord(false);
            return isLeafNode(node);
        }
        char ch = word.charAt(depth);
        boolean shouldDeleteNode = delete(node.getChild(ch), word, depth + 1);
        if (shouldDeleteNode) {
            node.setChild(ch, null);
            return isLeafNode(node);
        }
        return false;
    }
    private boolean isLeafNode(TrieNode node) {
        for (TrieNode child : node.children) {
            if (child != null) {
                return false;
            }
        }
        return true;
    }
}
public class TrieExample {
    public static void main(String[] args) {
        Trie trie = new Trie();
        trie.insert("apple");
        trie.insert("app");
        trie.insert("orange");
        System.out.println("Search 'apple': " + trie.search("apple")); // true
        System.out.println("Search 'app': " + trie.search("app")); // true
        System.out.println("Search 'orange': " + trie.search("orange")); // true
        System.out.println("Search 'banana': " + trie.search("banana")); // false
        System.out.println("Starts with 'app': " + trie.startsWith("app")); // true
```

```
        System.out.println("Starts with 'ban': " + trie.startsWith("ban")); // false
        trie.delete("apple");
        System.out.println("Search 'apple' after deletion: " + trie.search("apple")); // false
        System.out.println("Search 'app' after deletion: " + trie.search("app")); // true
    }
}
```

In this example:

- The TrieNode class represents a node in the Trie with an array of children nodes and a boolean flag indicating whether it is the end of a word.
- The Trie class contains methods for inserting, searching, and deleting strings in the Trie.
- The insert method inserts a string into the Trie, creating new nodes as needed.
- The search method checks if a string is present in the Trie.
- The startsWith method checks if there is any word in the Trie that starts with a given prefix.
- The delete method deletes a string from the Trie.
- The main method in the TrieExample class demonstrates the usage of the Trie by inserting, searching, and deleting words.

13.2. Use a trie implement an auto complete feature

Below is an example implementation of an autocomplete feature using a Trie data structure in Java. The TrieNode class represents a node in the Trie, and the AutocompleteTrie class provides methods for inserting words and performing autocomplete.

```
import java.util.ArrayList;
import java.util.List;
class TrieNode {
    private TrieNode[] children;
    private boolean isEndOfWord;
    public TrieNode() {
        this.children = new TrieNode[26]; // Assuming lowercase English letters
        this.isEndOfWord = false;
    }
    public TrieNode getChild(char ch) {
        return children[ch - 'a'];
    }
    public void setChild(char ch, TrieNode node) {
        children[ch - 'a'] = node;
    }
    public boolean isEndOfWord() {
        return isEndOfWord;
    }
    public void setEndOfWord(boolean endOfWord) {
        isEndOfWord = endOfWord;
    }
}
public class AutocompleteTrie {
    private TrieNode root;
    public AutocompleteTrie() {
        this.root = new TrieNode();
    }
    public void insert(String word) {
        TrieNode node = root;
```

```
        for (char ch : word.toCharArray()) {
            if (node.getChild(ch) == null) {
                node.setChild(ch, new TrieNode());
            }
            node = node.getChild(ch);
        }
        node.setEndOfWord(true);
    }
    public List<String> autocomplete(String prefix) {
        TrieNode node = searchNode(prefix);
        List<String> suggestions = new ArrayList<>();
        autocomplete(node, prefix, suggestions);
        return suggestions;
    }
    private TrieNode searchNode(String word) {
        TrieNode node = root;
        for (char ch : word.toCharArray()) {
            node = node.getChild(ch);
            if (node == null) {
                return null; // Prefix not found
            }
        }
        return node;
    }
    private void autocomplete(TrieNode node, String currentPrefix, List<String> suggestions)
{
        if (node == null) {
            return;
        }
        if (node.isEndOfWord()) {
            suggestions.add(currentPrefix);
        }
        for (char ch = 'a'; ch <= 'z'; ch++) {
```

```
            TrieNode child = node.getChild(ch);
            if (child != null) {
                autocomplete(child, currentPrefix + ch, suggestions);
            }
        }
    }
    public static void main(String[] args) {
        AutocompleteTrie trie = new AutocompleteTrie();
        trie.insert("apple");
        trie.insert("app");
        trie.insert("orange");
        trie.insert("banana");
        String prefix = "app";
        List<String> autocompleteSuggestions = trie.autocomplete(prefix);
        System.out.println("Autocomplete suggestions for prefix '" + prefix + "':");
        for (String suggestion : autocompleteSuggestions) {
            System.out.println(suggestion);
        }
    }
}
```

In this example:

- The AutocompleteTrie class contains methods for inserting words into the Trie and performing autocomplete for a given prefix.
- The autocomplete method performs autocomplete by traversing the Trie starting from the node corresponding to the given prefix.
- The main method demonstrates the usage of the autocomplete feature by inserting words into the Trie and retrieving autocomplete suggestions for the prefix "app".

14. ADVANCED TOPICS

14.1. Disjoint set data structure

A Disjoint Set (also known as Union-Find) is a data structure that keeps track of a partition of a set into disjoint subsets. Below is an example implementation of a Disjoint Set data structure in Java with a class named DisjointSet.

```
class DisjointSet {
    private int[] parent;
    private int[] rank;
    public DisjointSet(int size) {
        parent = new int[size];
        rank = new int[size];
        // Initialize each element as a separate set with rank 0
        for (int i = 0; i < size; i++) {
            parent[i] = i;
            rank[i] = 0;
        }
    }
    public int find(int x) {
        if (parent[x] != x) {
            // Path compression: Set the parent to the representative of the set
            parent[x] = find(parent[x]);
        }
        return parent[x];
    }
    public void union(int x, int y) {
        int rootX = find(x);
        int rootY = find(y);
        // Union by rank: Attach the smaller rank tree to the root of the larger rank tree
        if (rootX != rootY) {
            if (rank[rootX] < rank[rootY]) {
                parent[rootX] = rootY;
            } else if (rank[rootX] > rank[rootY]) {
                parent[rootY] = rootX;
```

```
            } else {
                parent[rootY] = rootX;
                rank[rootX]++;
            }
        }
    }
}
public class DisjointSetExample {
    public static void main(String[] args) {
        int size = 5;
        DisjointSet disjointSet = new DisjointSet(size);
        System.out.println("Initial Disjoint Set:");
        printSets(disjointSet);
        disjointSet.union(0, 1);
        disjointSet.union(2, 3);
        disjointSet.union(0, 4);
        System.out.println("Disjoint Set after unions:");
        printSets(disjointSet);
        // Find representative elements
        System.out.println("Find(0): " + disjointSet.find(0));
        System.out.println("Find(2): " + disjointSet.find(2));
        System.out.println("Find(3): " + disjointSet.find(3));
    }
    private static void printSets(DisjointSet disjointSet) {
        for (int i = 0; i < disjointSet.parent.length; i++) {
            System.out.println("Element " + i + ": Parent = " + disjointSet.parent[i] +
                    ", Rank = " + disjointSet.rank[i]);
        }
    }
}
```

In this example:

- The DisjointSet class contains methods for finding the representative of a set (find) and unioning two sets (union).

- Path compression is applied during the find operation to flatten the tree structure and improve the efficiency of subsequent find operations.
- Union by rank is used to keep the tree balanced, which helps to optimize the union operation.
- The main method demonstrates the usage of the DisjointSet by creating a disjoint set, performing union operations, and finding representative elements.
- Feel free to modify the size of the disjoint set and perform additional union operations to explore the behavior of the Disjoint Set data structure.

14.2. LRU cache

Below is an example implementation of an LRU (Least Recently Used) cache using a class in Java. The LRUCache class uses a combination of a doubly linked list and a HashMap to efficiently maintain the order of recently used elements.

```
import java.util.HashMap;
import java.util.Map;
class LRUCache {
    private final int capacity;
    private final Map<Integer, Node> cache;
    private final Node dummyHead;
    private final Node dummyTail;
    public LRUCache(int capacity) {
        this.capacity = capacity;
        this.cache = new HashMap<>();
        this.dummyHead = new Node(-1, -1);
        this.dummyTail = new Node(-1, -1);
        dummyHead.next = dummyTail;
        dummyTail.prev = dummyHead;
    }
    public int get(int key) {
        if (cache.containsKey(key)) {
            Node node = cache.get(key);
            // Move the accessed node to the front of the list
            moveToHead(node);
            return node.value;
        }
        return -1; // Key not found
    }
    public void put(int key, int value) {
        if (cache.containsKey(key)) {
            Node node = cache.get(key);
            // Update the value and move the node to the front of the list
            node.value = value;
```

```
            moveToHead(node);
        } else {
            if (cache.size() == capacity) {
                // Remove the least recently used node from the end of the list
                Node removedNode = removeTail();
                cache.remove(removedNode.key);
            }
            // Add a new node to the front of the list
            Node newNode = new Node(key, value);
            cache.put(key, newNode);
            addToHead(newNode);
        }
    }
    private void moveToHead(Node node) {
        removeNode(node);
        addToHead(node);
    }
    private void removeNode(Node node) {
        node.prev.next = node.next;
        node.next.prev = node.prev;
    }
    private void addToHead(Node node) {
        node.next = dummyHead.next;
        node.prev = dummyHead;
        dummyHead.next.prev = node;
        dummyHead.next = node;
    }
    private Node removeTail() {
        Node removedNode = dummyTail.prev;
        removeNode(removedNode);
        return removedNode;
    }
    private static class Node {
```

```
        int key;
        int value;
        Node prev;
        Node next;
        public Node(int key, int value) {
            this.key = key;
            this.value = value;
        }
    }
}
public class LRUCacheExample {
    public static void main(String[] args) {
        LRUCache lruCache = new LRUCache(2);
        lruCache.put(1, 1);
        lruCache.put(2, 2);
        System.out.println("Get(1): " + lruCache.get(1)); // Output: 1
        lruCache.put(3, 3);
        System.out.println("Get(2): " + lruCache.get(2)); // Output: -1 (not found)
        lruCache.put(4, 4);
        System.out.println("Get(1): " + lruCache.get(1)); // Output: -1 (not found)
        System.out.println("Get(3): " + lruCache.get(3)); // Output: 3
        System.out.println("Get(4): " + lruCache.get(4)); // Output: 4
    }
}
```

In this example:

- The LRUCache class contains methods for getting and putting values in the cache.
- The cache is implemented using a HashMap (cache) for quick lookups and a doubly linked list to maintain the order of recently used elements.
- The get method retrieves the value for a given key and moves the accessed node to the front of the list.
- The put method inserts or updates a key-value pair in the cache, ensuring that the capacity is not exceeded.
- The Node class represents a node in the doubly linked list.

- The main method demonstrates the usage of the LRUCache by inserting, retrieving, and updating values in the cache.

Feel free to adjust the cache capacity and test additional scenarios to explore the behavior of the LRU cache.

www.ingramcontent.com/pod-product-compliance
Lightning Source LLC
Chambersburg PA
CBHW040743170726
48282CB00023B/125
* 9 7 8 9 3 3 4 0 0 2 9 5 9 *